Contents

The Essential English Springer Spaniel

The English Springer Spaniel, with his wonderfully expressive head, is handsome, versatile and a marvellously devoted companion who simply adores the company of people. He is neither too large, nor too small, making him suitable to join in all sorts of activities. He is never happier than when helping his owner with something he considers an enjoyable pursuit. He is unfailingly enthusiastic and expresses his joy with a happily wagging tail, whether it be long or short.

Springer Spaniels are recorded among the very first sporting dogs – springing game for hounds and hawks to chase, and later for the gun.

THE ENGLISH SPRINGER'S ROOTS

The origin of the spaniel goes back a long while, but in those very early centuries of spaniel history, the breeds were not so clearly defined as they are today. It is likely that they were brought to Britain from Spain, by the Romans. The name 'spaniel' may be derived from the Basque word *'Espagna'* or maybe from *'Hispania'*, which is Latin for 'Spain'. Another possibility is that the name derives from the French verb *'s'espagner'*, which means 'to crouch'. No one will ever know for sure.

The spaniel was first mentioned in the Irish laws in AD17, referring to spaniels that had been given as tributes to the king. We know also that they came to Wales, where they were held in high regard by King 'Howell the Good' (King Howell Dha). In AD94, Spaniels were mentioned in Welsh laws and the esteem in which they were held is borne out by the fact that one single spaniel could buy several goats, geese, slaves, or even women.

In English literature the spaniel was mentioned by Geoffrey Chaucer in his *Canterbury Tales*, proving that the breed was certainly known in England over 600 years ago. In France, Gaston de Foix also brought the spaniel to people's attention in the 14th century in his famous *Livre de Chasse*. This feudal baron lived near the French/Spanish border and was convinced that the spaniel had its origin in Spain.

Another interesting reference to the spaniel came in the *Boke of St Albans*, written by Dame Juliana Berners in 1486. She was Prioress of Sopwell Nunnery in Hertfordshire and it is believed this book was written for the use of King Henry IV's son, to acquaint him with names of animals and terms used in venery and field sports.

In 1570 Dr Johannes Caius

Early Stud Records

Based in Shropshire, England, the Boughey family began its strain of Aqualate English Springer Spaniels in the year 1800. The family started its own stud book in 1812, which they kept going for over a century, retaining their interest in the breed until the 1930s, but sadly it seems none of the Aqualate dogs were ever registered with the Kennel Club. Charles Cyril Eversfield of Denne Park, Horsham, also kept stud records from the early 19th century and so it has been possible to trace back the lines behind notable dogs in the breed for many a long year.

Two dogs credited with possibly being the foundation of today's English Springer Spaniel are Mop I, born in 1812, and Frisk, to whom many of today's winning English Springers can be traced.

Mop was said to have possessed, in the highest degree, all those qualities that made a spaniel valuable: "a good nose, under excellent command, versatile in pursuit and equally good at either woodcock, pheasant, hare, rabbit, snipe or mallard. On land or in water, it was a matter of indifference to Mop which, if it was his master's wish, guided mentioned what he actually called Springer Spaniels in his highly acclaimed work *Treatise of Englishe Dogges* (this was first translated into English in 1576). He divided all sporting dogs into two, one for hunting beasts, the other for 'hunting' fowl; these he subdivided into land spaniels and those that found game on water. "The common sort of people," he said, "call them by one general word, namely, spaniels." Caius described them thus:

"The most part of their skin is white, and if they be marked with any spots, they are commonly red, and somewhat great therewithal, the hairs not growing in such thickness but that the mixture of

by the hand, checked by the whistle, indefatigable in his labours". Sadly, Mop's end came when he was accidentally killed.

Frisk had a pleasing countenance, "indicative of bustle and industry, qualities in the spaniel always desirable."

Mop and Frisk: These spaniels were the foundation of the breed we know today as the English Springer Spaniel.

*them may be easily perceived.
Other some of them be reddish and
blackish; but of that sort there be
but very few."*

Their work was springing game for
the hounds and hawks to chase. But
the many royal banquets in the days
of Henry VIII demanded so much
game such as rabbit, hare, quail,
pheasant and partridge, that a more
speedy method of catching was
implemented. This was 'netting',
which involved the spaniels driving
the birds in the direction of the
fowlers, who stood ready with their
nets. Not only the birds, but also the
dogs were caught under the nets,
and it is these who are the
ancestors of our modern day setter

breeds. Netting fell into disuse when
the gun was invented, allowing the
game to be caught by shooting.
Setting spaniels found the game and
pointed it, and the springers flushed
the game from cover, allowing it to
be shot.

Toy spaniels, which Caius called
the 'spaniel gentle' or 'comforter',
had been recognised in the 16th and
17th centuries, though they were
then larger and heavier than the Toy
Spaniel breeds so familiar to us
today. By the 18th century, the term
'Springing Spaniel' had come into
common usage, but for all Land
Spaniels, not for any particular
variety. By 1803 we learned from
Nicolas Cox in his *Sportsman's
Cabinet* that the larger spaniels were
known as Springing Spaniels and the
smaller ones, Cockers, or Cocking
Spaniels.

*The glamorous Irish
Setter was originally used
to find and 'point' game.*

THE SPANIEL FAMILY

English Springer Spaniel.

Welsh Springer Spaniel.

Cocker Spaniel

Cavalier King
Charles Spaniel.

Clumber Spaniel.

Field Spaniel.

Sussex Spaniel.

Irish Water Spaniel.

BREED RECOGNITION

For a while the breed was known as the 'Norfolk Spaniel', probably a misnomer brought about by the fact that it was kept by one of the Dukes of Norfolk. But when the breed was taken up by the Sporting Spaniel Society they decided to drop the name of 'Norfolk' and revert to the old title of 'Springer'.

Velox Powder: A successful show dog whose ancestry can be traced back to Mop and Frisk.

The English Springer Spaniel finally gained recognition by the English Kennel Club in 1902, more than a century after the Boughey family had begun keeping a stud book. But even then, classification for the breed at shows came about only occasionally and was divided into over 50 lbs in weight, and under 50 lbs but over 25 lbs. There were other permutations too, such as 'English Springer Spaniel other than Clumber or Sussex' and the unlikely classification of 'English Springer Spaniel (other than Clumber, Sussex or Field) old-fashioned, medium-legged spaniels, any colour'. Well, I suppose that narrowed down the field!

The Breed Standard had been drawn up by the Spaniel Club and before long Springers gained their titles as bench Champions. The very first Champion male was Beechgrove Will and the first bitch to gain her title was Fansom. Another important Springer to hit dizzy heights at that time was Velox Powder, who, incidentally, could be traced back 14 generations to Mop and Frisk. Powder became a Champion and won well in both the field and the show ring.

It was not unusual during the very early years of the 20th century for Springer Spaniel breeders to use other gundog breeds to fix 'type'. For example, an over-sized Cocker Spaniel bitch was mated to an English Springer Spaniel to produce the winning Springer, Ch. Rivington Sam, who was the first Field Trial Champion. English Springers and Pointers were also used, as were Clumber Spaniels, to improve bone; it is believed that Field Spaniels were also incorporated to improve heads.

The English Springer continued to be highly valued as a working dog.

the Kennel Club brought in the title of Field Trial Champion. Few English Springers gained their titles prior to the First World War, and during the war there was a lull in the show scene until the Scottish Kennel Club Show was staged in 1920. Until this time, the majority of fanciers were more interested in working their Springers than in showing them. However, the breed fared well during this difficult period, for not only was it a much-loved pet, but, by working, could also supplement the family food supply, which was especially useful for families based in the countryside between the two wars.

World War Two put an end to all showing activities and, as for all other breeds, it was a matter of survival. Breeding resumed after the war, but it took a while for the quality of the breed to return to pre-war levels. However, the English Springer Spaniel Club held its first post-war show in 1946.

As with several other breeds at that time, nomenclature and indeed breed names can be very confusing to follow. A daughter of Ch. Beechgrove Will was actually registered as a Field Spaniel, and orange-coloured puppies from an English Springer/English Setter mating were registered as Welsh Springer Spaniels. The mind boggles!

In those early years, the title of Champion could be gained either through shows or trials, but in 1909

The working Springer is now a distinct type and looks markedly different from those bred for the show ring.

THE BREED SPLITS IN TWO

It was around this time that a divergence appeared in the breed between the English Springers used for show, and those used for field trials. There are still people who believe that this was effectively the end of the truly 'dual purpose' English Springer Spaniel. Certainly, as the years have progressed, we have seen a considerable divergence in type between show dogs and those used for work. In general, those used in the field are somewhat smaller, with lighter bone, shorter ears and less feathering.

In the 1950s, the Kennel Club introduced the title of Show Champion for a dog that had won three Challenge Certificates (CCs) in the show ring, and Champion for one that had won three CCs but had also qualified in the field. The title of Dual Champion was for dogs that had won the title of Show Champion and also Field Trial Champion.

Several different breed representatives have made their mark and it is true that show and working enthusiasts have each bred to suit their personal preference. But one cannot overlook the breed record holder, Sh. Ch. Wadeson Inspector Wexford, who achieved the amazing tally of 61 CCs, 50 of these with Best of Breed awards. He died in 2007 at the age of eleven.

English Springers in America

It was reported early in the 17th century that there were two dogs on board the *Mayflower* used by the Pilgrim Fathers on their journey to New England. These were a Mastiff and a spaniel, giving rise to the theory that the spaniel, in some form or other, has been on that continent for a very long while. Indeed, the Springer Spaniel has long been popular in the USA where the breed has been used to work in swampland and in brambles. But, as setters became popular, the Springers decreased severely in numbers until they were threatened with extinction.

The American Spaniel Club was founded in 1880, when anything over 28 pounds in weight was called a Springer. But it was basically the Sporting Spaniel Society that saved the breed, for they decided to re-develop it using a variety of gundogs. These included the liver-and-white and black-and-white Keepers Spaniels, the Clumber and Sussex Spaniels, the Old English Water Spaniel, as well as Sportsmen's Setter and Spaniel crosses.

Their efforts were fruitful, and, with the help of imports from the UK, the genetic base was further widened. The Springer Spaniel, Denne Lucy, from the old Velox lines, was first officially registered in the USA in 1910, but it took until 1923 for a show to be held offering classes for the breed. The English Springer Spaniel Field Trial Association (ESSFTA) was founded in Fishers Island, New York in 1924 when the first US field trial was held. The ESSFTA was named the parent club of the breed in 1927 and is still in existence today. In 1927 the American Kennel Club recognised the Breed Standard for the English Springer Spaniel, but this was replaced by another in 1932.

Even the briefest early history of the breed in the USA would not be complete without mention of Mr Eudore Chevrier whose home was in Manitoba, Canada. In the short space of three and a half years, he imported 250 dogs from England, including Champions. By 1925 he had 600 Springers in his kennels and it is clear that he played a large part in establishing the breed's popularity both in Canada and the USA.

Later, during the 1950s and 1960s, many high-quality examples of the breed were also imported to the United States from Britain, helping the breed to prosper still further. But, as in Britain, a variance in type developed between those dogs destined for the show ring and those whose talents lay in the field. In addition to this, the English Springer Spaniel

Top-quality stock was exported to establish the breed in the USA.

exhibited at shows in the United States developed along very different lines from those in the UK, so that now there is a very obvious difference between them.

Most Springers in the USA are either black-and-white or liver-and-white, without any ticking. They tend to be smaller than those in Britain and are more like the Cocker Spaniel in head; they also tend to carry more coat. In fact, the breed has become so different in the USA that many fanciers have suggested that it should now be registered under a different name.

The English Springers in North America today excel not only in conformation classes – Ch. Felicity's Diamond Jim won Best in Show at the prestigious Westminster Show in 2007 – but also in obedience, agility, tracking, hunting tests and field trials, so they must surely rank among one of the most versatile dogs in existence.

THE BREED STANDARD

A Breed Standard is effectively a picture painted in words, providing breeders, judges, exhibitors and enthusiasts with a verbal 'portrait' of what they should be striving for, or hoping to find. But there is no perfect dog and everyone's interpretation of a Standard varies slightly, which is why many different dogs win top honours in the show ring; in short, they are being judged by different judges.

The Breed Standard has had certain revisions over the years, the last of which in the UK was in December 2008. A major change in the Standards for many breeds came about in the mid-1980s, by which time the Kennel Club had taken over responsibility for all Breed Standards. In their endeavour to have uniformity of format across the breeds, substantial changes were made, with lengthy prior consultation with the breed clubs. In the most recent revisions there has, sadly, been less open discussion.

Now all Breed Standards in the UK are prefaced with the following statement:

"A Breed Standard is the guideline which describes the ideal characteristics, temperament and appearance of a breed and ensures that the breed is fit for function. Absolute soundness is essential. Breeders and judges should at all times be careful to avoid obvious conditions or exaggerations which would be detrimental in any way to the health, welfare or soundness of this breed. From time to time certain conditions or exaggerations may be considered to have the potential to affect dogs in some breeds adversely, and judges and breeders are requested to refer to the Kennel Club website for details of any such current issues. If a feature or quality is desirable, it should only be present in the right measure."

General appearance

The English Springer Spaniel is a strong, symmetrically built dog, the highest on the leg and raciest in build of all the British land spaniels, the others being the American Cocker, Cocker, Clumber, Field, Sussex and Welsh Springer Spaniels. All these breeds fall within the Gundog group in the UK.

This breed is also compact and is built for endurance, for although classed as a land spaniel, he is also happy in water, from which he will willingly retrieve. An active breed, he has an enormous amount of stamina and gives one the impression that he could keep going all day. Even under 'General Appearance' the Breed Standard describes him as "merry", indicating that his happy personality shines through in his appearance.

POINTS OF ANATOMY

Skull
Occiput
Crest
Stop
Neck
Shoulder
Withers
Loin
Croup
Muzzle
Stifle
Flews
Chest
Tail
Foreleg
Hock
Wrist
Flank
Front foot
Lower thigh
Pastern
Hind foot
Elbow

Characteristics

This is one of the oldest of the sporting gundogs, whose original purpose was to find and spring game for the net, hound or falcon, but today the working English Springer is used to find, flush and retrieve game for the gun. He is often referred to as a 'Jack of all trades', for this is the perfect working companion for those who go out on a shoot. When he approaches dense cover he has no fear, and his scenting and hunting abilities are first rate. The English Springer is responsive and eager to please, added to which he can retrieve tenderly to hand, making him a great all-rounder.

Temperament

With his friendly, happy, biddable disposition, the English Springer is renowned for his love of people, enjoying the company of both adults and children. He generally loves life itself, and is usually happy in the company of other dogs, too. The English Springer Spaniel should show

This is a breed that has a great joy of life and loves being with people.

no signs of timidity or aggression, but owners should recognise that any dog, if treated unkindly, can undergo a change in personality – something to be avoided at all costs.

Head and skull

The English Springer has a medium-length skull, which is fairly broad and slightly rounded, without a prominent occiput. As the skull rises from the foreface, it makes a stop and groove, also known as 'fluting' between the eyes; this gradually disappears at the middle of the forehead. The stop is not a deep one, but might be described as moderate.

Although the eyebrows are well defined, they are not heavy, and the delicate moulding under the eyes adds refinement to the head. The cheeks are flat. The beauty of this breed's head is enhanced by the fact that the foreface is proportionate to the length of skull and is fairly broad and deep. In a breed with working abilities, it is especially important that the nostrils are well developed.

The American Breed Standard has the following highly descriptive paragraph describing the cheeks and jaw:

"The cheeks are flat, and the face is well-chiselled below the eyes. Jaws are of sufficient length to allow the dog to carry game easily; fairly square, lean and strong. The upper lips come down full and rather square to cover the line of the lower jaw, however, the lips are never pendulous or exaggerated."

Eyes

In America it is said that the English Springer Spaniel's eyes, more than any other feature, are the essence of the breed's appeal, and I feel sure many enthusiasts on this side of the Atlantic feel the same way. He has a soft, trusting, intelligent expression.

The eyes should be of medium size and almond-shaped, neither prominent nor sunken. They are deeply set in the sockets and should show no haw – something that would leave them exposed to invasion of grass seeds when working. Although it is not mentioned in the English Breed Standard, the eyes should be set fairly wide apart. The correct colour is dark hazel; light eyes are undesirable, as they completely change the warmth of the expression. It is generally accepted, however, that colour does vary slightly according to coat colour: black-and-white dogs tend to have a darker eye than liver-and-whites.

The soft, trusting expression is so typical of the breed.

The American Standard requires eye rims to be fully pigmented and to match the coat colour. Although this is not specifically mentioned in the UK Standard, it is generally accepted that this should be the case in the UK, too.

Ears

The English Springer's ears are of good length and width, the leather being approximately long enough to reach the tip of the nose, but they should not be so long that they interfere with the ability to move freely and quickly when scenting. They hang fairly close to the sides of the head and are set in line with the outer corner of the eye.

The long ears should not interfere with the Springer's ability to move freely.

Mouth

The strong jaw should have a perfect, regular and complete scissor bite, meaning that the upper teeth closely overlap the lower ones and are set square to the jaws. The American Standard is more lenient, also allowing for an even bite (edge to edge) and if one or two incisors are slightly out of line, it is considered only a minor fault. More severe deviations are considered serious faults that are to be heavily penalised.

It is important that the English Springer can carry game easily and squarely. In the UK all bites other than a scissor bite are penalised in the show ring, even though they do not necessarily affect a dog's ability to retrieve efficiently.

Neck

The neck is strong, muscular and of good length, which is essential if this breed is to do its work efficiently. The English Springer must be able to hold his nose just above ground when moving, but when carrying heavy game the neck must be sufficiently strong to support the head comfortably. The length of neck should be roughly the same as the length of the head; too short and it would interfere with the dog's ability to retrieve, too long and it would lack sufficient strength.

The Standard asks for the neck to be "slightly arched, tapering towards the head" and also "free from throatiness", which is important, as loose folds of skin would be prone to injury.

Forequarters

As might be expected in a dog of these proportions, the forelegs are straight and should be well boned, generally described as 'flat round' in shape.

The sloping shoulders are well laid,

The forelegs are straight and the elbows are set close to the body.

in keeping with the long neck; the shoulder blade and upper arm should be of roughly the same length. This allows the legs to be set well under the body. Elbows are set well to the body. The English Springer needs strong, flexible pasterns.

Body

The English Springer Spaniel has a strong body that is neither too long nor too short; it should be just slightly longer than high, yet should still appear compact. The deep chest is well developed and the ribs well sprung, allowing plenty of heart-room and lung capacity, but it should not be so wide that it impedes function and causes the forelegs to be anything other than straight. The loin should be muscular and strong, with a slight arch. The English Springer is well coupled, meaning that the distance between the ribs and pelvis should be fairly short in order to provide strength, and yet it needs also to be sufficiently long to allow some flexibility.

In the American Standard we learn that the hips are nicely rounded,

The body is slightly longer than it is high.

blending smoothly into the hind legs, the croup sloping gently to the set of the tail.

Hindquarters

It is important to remember that the Springer Spaniel's propulsion comes from the hindquarters, so everything needs to fit together correctly and be balanced to match the forequarters. The hindlegs are well let down, the stifles and hocks moderately bent, and the broad thighs muscular and well developed; this applies to both first and second thighs. If there is a relatively short distance between the hock joint and ground, this will provide greater drive.

Tail

Until the spring of 2007, the English Springer Spaniel's tail was customarily docked in the UK, to approximately two-thirds of its normal length. The reason for this was to reduce the risk of injury when working in thick cover, for the tip of the tail is fine and therefore particularly vulnerable. But now, under the terms of the Animal Welfare Act, docking is not allowed. There are, however, exemptions to this for working gundogs, but not in Scotland, where there is a total ban.

Whether docked or otherwise, the tail is set on low and is never carried above the level of the back. It is well

Feet

The feet should be tight and compact, well rounded with strong, full pads. Often they are described as 'cat-like', for these are the Springer Spaniel's shock absorbers but are also sufficiently flexible to work on rough terrain. Because the front feet carry the greatest proportion of the dog's weight, they tend to be a little larger than the hind feet. Dewclaws should be removed within a few days of birth, so they will not become damaged when working.

feathered with a lively action, and, in the case of complete tails, should be in balance with the rest of the dog.

In America the English Springer's tail may be carried horizontally or slightly elevated, but never so high as to be at a right angle to the backline.

Movement

When moving, the English Springer Spaniel's forelegs swing straight forward from the shoulder. The feet are thrown well forward in an easy, free manner. In the rear, the hocks drive well under the body, following

Traditionally the tail was docked.

The tail – which is now full length – should be in balance with the rest of the dog.

the same line as the forelegs. Although generally frowned upon in the show ring, when moving at a slow pace there may be a pacing movement.

If an English Springer Spaniel is soundly constructed, movement will be effortless, covering the ground with economy and style. Structural faults will result in untypical movement.

Coat

For a working dog like the English Springer Spaniel, a topcoat and undercoat are essential for protection; the topcoat carries oil, which acts as a barrier against water. The UK Breed Standard simply describes it as: "Close, straight and weather resisting never coarse", which probably puts it in a nutshell, but is far less explicit than the American Standard, which explains that the outercoat is flat or wavy and is easily distinguishable from the short, soft, dense undercoat. In the USA, as, of course, in Britain, the quantity of undercoat is affected by climate and season.

The English Springer has moderate feathering on ears, forelegs, body and hindquarters, but this should never be so long that it interferes with the dog's working ability in the field. In actual fact, the feathering was originally intended to protect the dog's vulnerable areas from injury.

The English Springer should cover the ground with economy and style.

English Springer Colours

Liver and white.

Liver and white with tan markings.

Colour

The striking colours of the English Springer Spaniel are highly attractive; they are either black-and-white or liver-and-white, either of which may have tan markings, in which case it is a tri-colour.

Technically, any amount of any colour may be present, but in theory show dogs tend to carry more colour than dogs that are used only for working. In the show ring, a dog considered to have 'classical markings' has a jacket of solid colour, white legs, collar and front of neck, while the head and ears are of solid colour with a white blaze, or flash from the muzzle to the forehead. The muzzle is also usually white. Ticking is allowed in any amount on the body, legs and muzzle.

When tan is present, it is primarily on the eyebrows, lower

Black and white.

Black and white with tan markings.

cheeks and under the tail, and there are often tan spots among the ticking on the muzzle and legs.

Size

The UK Breed Standard states clearly and simply that the approximate height is 51 cms (20 ins), while the American Standard goes into meticulous specifics and also mentions weight, which should be 50 pounds (22.5 kgs) for a 20-inch dogs and 40 pounds (18.8 kgs) for a 19-inch (48.3 cms) bitch. The American Standard says the ideal height for a male is 20 inches and for a female 19 inches, but provided they are not more than one inch over or under the ideal height, this is not to be faulted.

In Britain the Standard used also to contain a weight clause, which

English Springers from working lines have less feathering and often carry less colour than dogs from show lines.

Standard; there is merely a clause in which it states that "the seriousness with which the fault should be regarded should be in exact proportion to its degree." It is essentially for the judge to decide how seriously the fault reflects on the overall merit, or otherwise, of the dog being exhibited.

In the American Standard faults are incorporated in each relevant section of the Standard, with indication as to whether they are serious, not so serious, or disqualifying faults.

In Britain every Breed Standard requires a male to have two apparently normal testicles fully descended into the scrotum. Having said that, the Kennel Club has actually specified that it is now possible to exhibit neutered dogs and bitches, but, in reality, few males are shown if they do not have both testicles descended.

was 50 lbs (22.5 kgs), and it is generally accepted that bitches are a little smaller and correspondingly lighter in weight.

Faults and notes

In Britain individual faults are no longer listed in any Breed

SUMMING UP

When assessing any pedigree breed, just by looking at a dog you should know what breed it is. It is breed 'type' that shows you that an English Springer Spaniel is indeed an English Springer. A dog may be soundly constructed, which is good, but if he looks more like a Clumber Spaniel, a Field Spaniel, an Irish Red and White Setter or even an Afghan Hound, then he is lacking 'breed type', so something is seriously wrong and he does not meet the requirements of the Breed Standard.

Yes, a soundly constructed dog may move absolutely beautifully, but he must have that certain 'something' that tells you he is an English Springer Spaniel through and through. But to be typical of his breed, he should also be sound, both in body and mind. Let us never forget the description of his temperament, which is: "Friendly, happy disposition, biddable. Timidity or aggression highly undesirable."

The essence of a top-quality dog is breed type – meaning that it looks like an English Springer Spaniel and no other breed.

Certainly we can forgive a touch of timidity in a young puppy, especially when he is exposed to new surroundings and situations for the very first time, but he should soon overcome this quickly and with ease, so that he matures into a confident adult that endears himself to all.

Choosing An English Springer Spaniel

H opefully, before deciding to buy an English Springer Spaniel, you will have done plenty of research on the breed so that you are as certain as you possibly can be that this is the right breed for you, and for your family. You can expect your English Springer to live into double figures, so this is not a commitment you can take lightly.

The English Springer is an energetic breed, so you will need to provide an outlet for his energy.

There are many, many breeds of dog out there from which to choose, so although the English Springer may have taken your initial fancy, look into some other breeds, too, for it may be that there is another breed that would fit in better with your own circumstances. I am certainly not trying to put you off buying a Springer, I just want you to be certain that this is the breed you plan to have living with you for at the next decade, possibly up to 14 years. Sadly, too many dogs of all breeds end up in rescue homes, purely because their owners have done too little research before purchasing a puppy and have probably allowed their hearts to rule their heads.

THE PROS AND CONS

There are probably many reasons why the English Springer Spaniel is exactly right for you, but there may also be reasons why he is not.

Let us look first at size and coat. This is a medium-sized breed, but still fairly substantial; he is a powerfully built dog that stands up to 51 cms (20 ins) at the shoulder and weighs up to 22.5 kgs (50 lbs). Firstly, you must ask yourself whether you can really cope with a dog of this size. Might he be too strong for you and pull you, or too big and bouncy if you have small children? This is an active breed, and although a Springer will jump into the back of the car rather than be lifted in, it may be a different story when he grows old, so do think ahead.

Although his coat is not as long as those of some breeds, it is still considerable, and is a double coat to protect the dog from the elements. This means that it does entail some work on your part. An English Springer's coat that is not regularly attended to with at least the occasional bath will end up causing discomfort to your dog and will be smelly to boot! English Springers are essentially 'outdoor types'; this is a breed that was originally bred as a working dog, so he loves to run in fields and roll in as many smelly droppings as he can find – the smellier the better! So if you want a pleasant-smelling, good-looking household companion, you will definitely need to pay regular attention to the coat.

You should consider whether or not an English Springer Spaniel will be too energetic for you. Although he can be quiet and calm, this is a working dog and so he has an abundance of energy and a lively mind, too. You will need to keep both body and mind sufficiently occupied. But if you are

Dog or Bitch?

You may have a personal preference for a male or female dog, perhaps because you have had a bitch before and would like another female companion to join you, or you may just have a soft spot for bitches, or indeed males. The decision may well be made purely because you instantly fall in love with a particular puppy in a litter, but if you know in your heart of hearts that it is one particular sex or the other that you crave, think double-hard before you make your final choice.

In general, a male ends up larger than a female and is therefore both heavier and stronger, so you may wish to take this into consideration. A male may be slightly harder to manage from the time he undergoes a hormonal change at about seven months old until he gets through the 'junior' stage. A male will also frequently lift his leg and leave his 'mark', just to let every other male in the vicinity know he is around. When testosterone levels are high, he may not be friendly with other males, so you will need to exercise firm control. But males are great characters, usually devoted to their owners and always easy to please.

Bitches are generally less wilful and many owners say they are more biddable, but again, when hormonal changes are at work they can succumb to mood changes. Also, around the time of a season, a bitch's coat will tend the outdoor type, who loves a long hike in the countryside, or if you want to get involved in field sports, the English Springer is probably exactly the right breed for you.

Certainly your home environment will play a large part in determining your suitability as an owner of an English Springer. If you live in a high-rise block of flats without a garden, I am afraid that this will not be the sort of place where an English Springer Spaniel would like to live, however much you may adore the breed. You will need to have a garden and, ideally, easy access to a field or

to moult – something that will happen roughly twice a year.

Some people say that when dogs and bitches are neutered it will change their personality and they will become easier to manage, but this rarely appears to be the case in reality.

The male (left) is generally bigger than the female (right).

paddock, even if that might involve a short trip in car. Just keep in mind that your car will need to be of the 'practical' kind, for you are sure to have a lot of muddy paw marks in the back on the return journey!

If you have children in your family, you will find that an English Springer Spaniel will generally get along well with all family members. However, you must teach your children to be kind to your dog, allowing him free space when he needs it. If an English Springer has been working in the field, or has returned from a long, energetic walk, he will probably want to relax quietly at home, so do not let your children pester him when he is enjoying a well-deserved rest.

SHOW, WORKING OR PET?

Because the English Springer Spaniel was bred as a working dog, you may well decide that it is a true working dog that will best suit your needs and environment. In this case you would be best advised to purchase a puppy that comes from a litter going back to working lines, in which their ancestors, including their sire and dam, have been trained to the gun. Working dogs are often smaller, finer in bone and their ears are higher set. They will also have less feathering and there are noticeable differences in the head type – the working Springer tending to have a

English Springers bred from working lines require mental stimulation as well as physical activity.

broader, flatter skull and being less square in muzzle than a show dog of this breed.

The show world is a very different one from that of field trials and the working dog. Sometimes the barriers are crossed and the show enthusiast plays a role in the working world too, but this is the exception rather than the rule. In part this is due to the considerable difference in the construction of the two 'types' of English Springer, despite the fact that they share the same name. Generally the show dog works at a slower pace, the working dog having been bred for speed and intelligence, not merely conformation to breed type.

Both working and show dogs come in the same colours, so if your English Springer is to be purely a pet, you will probably just choose the dog whose appearance appeals to you. But please bear in mind that any English Springer Spaniel needs to be kept active in mind and body, more especially one that come from working lines. Whichever you choose, you should also consider that however suitable a dog appears to be for the show ring, the gun, or just as a pet, a lot will depend on how he is brought up and trained, and how much effort you, his owner, have put in.

MORE THAN ONE
Obviously if you only plan to keep one dog, whatever the sex, life will not be too difficult; even when a bitch comes into season you will just have to take care that she is kept away from other dogs. However, if you keep both sexes in your home, you must have some provision to keep males and females apart when necessary. It is

English Springers mix well together – these dogs are from a 'girls only' household.

Living with other pets

Providing they have been socialised correctly, most English Springers get along well with other animals, and this applies both to those worked in the field and for show. Although a dog that is kept with another in a travelling crate may give the occasional warning growl, in a working test any exhibition of bad behaviour would not be tolerated. An adult may also show dominance over a youngster, but this is not usually a problem; he is just establishing his authority so the youngster knows his place.

How well, or otherwise, an English Springer gets along with other household pets can vary, but working dogs with strong hunting instincts are more likely to object to them than show dogs or pets. Sometimes, as can happen with many breeds, a dog seems to know the cats, rabbits and so forth belonging to his family, and will behave well with them, whereas he will be all too ready to chase the neighbour's cat, especially if it turns up unexpectedly in his garden!

Careful introduction and supervision is essential, and this should be undertaken at an early age. If you have adopted the right attitude with your dog, so he knows who is boss, there is a fair chance that your English Springer will learn to get along well with your other four-legged family friends.

important to remember that a dog who really wants to get to a bitch when she is at the peak of her season will go to almost any lengths to do so.

When the males in your canine family have no bitches in season to worry about, harmony will be restored and they will all get along happily together, no matter how many you have. However, it is worth noting that it is not recommended to take on two youngsters at exactly the same time, such as two from the same litter.

AN OLDER DOG

Taking on an older dog can sometimes be just as much hard work as introducing a new puppy to the household, although a lot will depend on the older dog's background, how he has been trained and how big a change he has to make to adapt to his new life.

It may be that you have just decided to take on an older puppy or 'junior' – one who has been run on by a breeder but who has not turned out as expected as a potential show or working dog. In this case all the puppy's 'teething troubles' will be over; he will have been vaccinated and, hopefully, house-trained and socialised. However, he will have to get used to a new routine and new toileting arrangements, so he will need time to adjust and re-learn, to a certain extent.

Another possibility is to be put into contact with a breeder who has a bitch whose breeding days are over, and so needs a new home, or it may be that she has had medical problems and has had to be spayed. Some of us cannot bear to part with our dogs, whether or not they will be of future use to our breeding programmes, but there are others who believe this type of dog will get a better, loving life with a new family, where she will get plenty of attention. This arrangement will usually work out well, but again you must give the lady time to adapt to her new situation.

Yet another way of getting hold of an older English Springer Spaniel is to arrange to take on a rescued dog, if one is available. Sadly, many English Springers now end up in 'rescue' due, in no small part, to the fact that the breed is now so popular. Many people take on a Springer without having given it sufficient

There are often valid reasons as to why a dog needs rehoming.

thought beforehand, later finding the dog does not fit in with their family circumstances. It may be that a new child has come on the scene and, all too often, people decide the family pet has to go. This is especially sad because English Springers generally get along well with children. Sometimes people realise too late that the English Springer is a more exuberant breed than they had envisaged and do not have sufficient time or energy to cope with his needs.

There are sometimes unavoidable reasons for rehoming, such as when the owner might have died or been taken into a long-term care home where dogs are not allowed. This is very sad because in such cases the dog will most probably have lived a very happy life with his former owner and will not understand the reason for the parting. In such circumstances, it may take a dog a good while to adjust, but if you are the right prospective owner, you will have patience and will have the satisfaction of knowing that you gave a lonely English Springer the best possible last few years of his life.

To locate a rescued dog, your first port of call should be to an English Springer Spaniel breed club secretary, whose number can usually be located via the internet, or alternatively through the Kennel Club. Through the secretary, you can be put in touch with those who deal with or run the rescue wing of the club. Another avenue might be via one of the larger rescue societies that deal with all breeds, as occasionally English Springers may end up there.

EXERCISE NEEDS

An English Springer Spaniel is not a breed that will be happy leading a

A puppy will get as much exercise as he needs playing in the garden.

sedentary life. This will lead also to an unfit, unhealthy pet that is lacking in both physical and mental stimulation, which should be considered essential. An English Springer needs plenty of free exercise, preferably somewhere really exciting, such as in a wood or a field with lots to stimulate his senses. This will also allow him the opportunity to develop his hunting instincts.

The English Springer Spaniel puppy, however, should not be given too much exercise. If you have a sizeable garden, this will be sufficient area in which to exercise a puppy up to the age of six months. In addition, you could take him on a short lead walk, provided he is fully vaccinated. This will allow you to socialise him, both with other dogs and with people. His walks should gradually be increased so that by the age of around nine months he is getting about an hour-long walk each day. Then, once he has reached his first birthday, you will find he has an abundance of energy and will appreciate as much exercise as you can give him.

Even though your Springer may not be used as a working dog, he will still have similar natural instincts, so you should allow him to find and retrieve objects, giving him plenty of praise and encouragement when he brings them back to you. This will give him great joy – and you, too!

Always bear in mind that if any dog is provided with insufficient exercise and mental stimulation, he will create his own entertainment, and this might well be chewing through a chair leg or doing other serious damage around the house. So often a so-called 'destructive dog' is only destructive because his owners have allowed him to become so.

The English Springer thrives on mental and physical activity.

Ideally, you will see the puppies when they are at their most active.

FINDING AN ENGLISH SPRINGER PUPPY

Unless you already know a breeder of English Springer Spaniels – someone you trust and from whom you are prepared to wait for a litter – you will need to start your search for a puppy through a reliable source. Breed club secretaries usually keep a list of breeders who have puppies available and, because these people are members of their clubs, they will have a fair idea of whether or not they are reputable breeders who have the English Springer's best interests at heart. You certainly do not want to buy your puppy from someone who is 'only in it for the money' and, regrettably, there are some so-called 'breeders' of that ilk around.

If you have easy access to the internet, you will be able to pick up details of most breed clubs from there, but another way of getting hold of useful telephone numbers is by ringing the Kennel Club (KC). There is now a scheme whereby people who technically abide by a set of rules that have been laid down by the KC become 'Kennel Club Accredited Breeders', but please be aware that some less-than-reputable breeders can find their way into this scheme by circumventing the rules. On the other hand, there are many excellent breeders out there who simply do not agree with the scheme, so are not members. Basically it will be down to you to decide who is, and who is not, a good breeder. All you can do is take sound advice where you can.

If you want a puppy essentially for the show ring, a breed club secretary will guide you to someone who has successful show stock, but if you want a working dog, they will put you in touch with the club's Field Trial section.

VIEWING THE PUPPIES

When you first make contact with breeders who have puppies available, or bitches due to whelp, you will probably be bombarded with questions over the phone. This is a good thing. The breeder is trying to ascertain at an early stage whether or not you would be a suitable owner for one of his puppies. Equally, you will have numerous questions you will want to ask the breeder, so when you call, make sure you have plenty of time to have a lengthy chat.

It is unlikely that a breeder will allow you to view the puppies until they are about four weeks old. By this time they will be up on their legs and starting to become less dependent on their mother. They will have also begun the weaning process, so the mother will be a little less possessive of them.

When the time comes that you do go along to visit, try to be punctual and make sure you are wearing clean clothes that have not come into contact with other dogs. If you are allowed to touch the puppies, you may be asked to

wash your hands before you do so. Do not take offence; the puppies will not yet have had any of their vaccinations at this age and are vulnerable to infection. If there are children in your family, it would be wise to leave the at home on this, your first visit. Children can be very persuasive, and you will need to make an unbiased appraisal of the litter and about the suitability of having one of the puppies. All puppies look cute, but if you have any reservations about the breeder, the cleanliness of the surroundings, or the health or quality of the litter, you must stand your ground and say

It is important to see the mother with her puppies so you will get an idea of the temperament they are likely to inherit.

"no", and continue searching until you find the right puppy.

If you are visiting a dam with young puppies, do not be surprised if she is a little protective of them; this is only natural. From a distance, take a very careful look at all the puppies in the litter and quietly observe their behaviour. You will not wish to select a puppy that is shy, and certainly not one that is aggressive. When the pups are a little older – perhaps on your second visit – they should have developed sufficiently in personality to come to you when you attract them. This is the time at which you will probably decide which one is for you. Colour and markings may also play a part in your decision but personality should be of prime importance.

If you are seeking a puppy for the show ring, you will also have to evaluate how the puppy matches up to the Breed Standard. If you are a newcomer to the breed, you need to take the breeder's advice on this, as well as checking that both the sire and the dam are of sufficiently high quality. It is unlikely that the sire is on the premises, but the breeder will, hopefully, have a photo available for you to look at, or maybe he is featured on an internet site.

If your requirement is for a working dog, you will have made extensive enquiries into the working abilities of the sire and the dam and, if possible, of other close relations. If you are choosing an English Springer Spaniel purely as a pet, of course you will want one that looks typical of the breed, but the main thing you will need to consider is temperament. In any event, you will not be able to collect your puppy from the breeder until he is at least eight weeks old;

The breeder will help you to assess show potential.

indeed some breeders prefer not to let puppies go to their new homes until the ninth or tenth week.

Always check if there will be any restrictions laid down by the breeder. It may be that the Kennel Club registration certificate is endorsed, stating that the dog or bitch cannot be used for breeding. This can be done because the breeder wishes to preserve her own breeding lines, or because it is felt that the puppy will not turn out to be of sufficiently high quality to be bred from.

Whichever your reason for purchasing an English Springer Spaniel puppy, before you make your final decision, you must be sure you are entirely captivated, for the puppy you take home with you should remain with you for life.

Choosing a show puppy

The puppy you see at only a few weeks of age will not look like an exact replica of his sire or dam. He will have a lot of growing to do, and different parts of his anatomy will develop at different rates. The breeder should offer to stand each of the potential show puppies four-square on a table. This will enable her to go over the various points of the dog so that you can see how well, or otherwise, they are likely to develop.

If you have a friend who is knowledgeable about the breed, it may be a good idea to take this person along with you to offer a second opinion – but always ask the breeder if she has any objection. However experienced the person you take along with you, different lines of breeding invariably develop in different ways at different rates. This is all the more reason why, if you are seeking a puppy with show potential, you should purchase from a breeder who has an in-depth knowledge of the breed and of their own breeding lines.

Lastly, no one should offer you a 'show puppy' – there is no such thing – at least not at the tender age of only a few weeks old. The puppy still has a lot of developing to do, which will determine the eventual outcome of his quality. A puppy may have 'show potential', and any genuine breeder will only sell you a puppy on this understanding.

Health issues

The English Springer Spaniel is generally a healthy breed but, as with most breeds, there are a few hereditary conditions that are breed related. It is therefore important to check that the sire and dam have all the health clearances that relate to breed-specific conditions.

Information on health conditions relating to English Springer Spaniels is given in Chapter Six: Health Care.

Settling In

Well before you are due to bring your new English Springer home, you should have done a lot of preparation and groundwork to be sure that everything is in place for his arrival. You should have planned out where he is to sleep, where he is to learn to relieve himself, and you need to buy all the equipment that will be needed for at least the first few weeks.

GARDEN SAFETY

The first thing you will need to check is the garden, which must be ultra-safe. It is surprising how an inquisitive puppy can wriggle through the smallest gap to the great wide world beyond – and that world may not be a safe place. Check that the gate is secure and, if necessary, erect a second gate so there is no means of accidental escape. Not every visitor to your house will know you have a dog, so it would be wise to erect a sign, urging people to keep the gate closed. If you have a wrought-iron gate, you may temporarily need to put a mesh covering on it, for a small puppy might be able to squeeze through, even though it may not look possible.

English Springer puppies are great explorers so you must check that your garden is both safe and secure.

Fencing must be sufficiently high for your dog not to be able to jump over it; six feet (1.83 metres) high is ideal, for you should consider that something a puppy would not be able to scale might be more easily cleared by an adult. When checking fences, look carefully at the bottom to be sure that shrubs are not hiding pieces of loose or broken fencing.

A garden is a wonderful and exciting place for a dog, but it can be full of hazards, too. Ponds can present a danger, so until your Springer is older, it would be wise to erect some sort of guard or to cover the pond, unless you plan to supervise him whenever he is in the garden. If you have a terrace with an unprotected steep drop, this will also need some adjustment, as a puppy could easily run right over the edge when he is playing.

Keep all weedkillers, slug pellets and chemicals well out of harm's way on a high shelf in a shed. Storing them inside the shed is not enough, as a puppy is so quick that he can easily slip in unnoticed. You should also think about any poisonous plants that may be growing in your garden, and either remove them (sad though that may be) or protect them. For a full list of poisonous plants, log on to the internet.

IN THE HOME

Inside the house, the same storage rule applies to chemicals, kitchen and bathroom cleaners, medicines, and children's toys that may cause danger to your puppy and upset to your child if they are chewed or swallowed. Exposed electrical cables are another potential hazard; many a puppy has quietly chewed though the plastic casing before exposing, probably days later, the wires beneath. You may also need to move some of your precious ornaments up to a higher level, both for your puppy's sake and for that of the ornaments!

Unless you live in a bungalow, you will also need to consider how to protect your puppy from accidents on the stairs. The easiest way is to erect a baby gate or dog gate at the bottom so that he simply cannot reach the stairs. This can be easily dismantled later if, when he is older, you decide to allow him the free run of the house. Indeed, you may decide to move it to the kitchen door when he grows a bit taller, so that he can be kept out of the kitchen when you are preparing a hot meal, or when you have visitors. I always find it useful to have one of these gates stored away in the garage ready for use when required.

An adult Springer will appreciate his own cosy bed – and it can be easily cleaned when necessary.

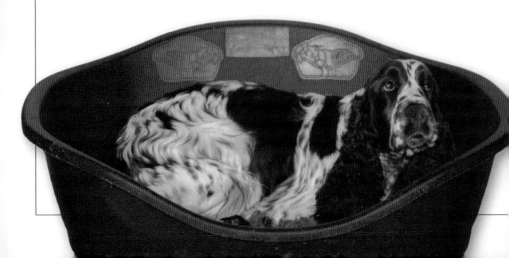

EQUIPMENT TO BUY

Well, you will probably have had to lay out a good deal of cash to buy your puppy and you will be spending a lot more in the pet shop before his arrival – so be warned!

Dog bed

Your puppy will need a special place of his own, and this will mean buying him his own bed. I find the strong, plastic type is best, as they are already slightly raised from the ground and can easily be hosed down in the garden, something that is likely to happen all too often considering a Springer Spaniel's potentially muddy feet. The bed should be lined with a veterinary fleece, of which you will need two pieces cut to size (so one can be used while the other is washed). Buy a bed of more than comfortable size, as your puppy will grow quickly, but you will almost certainly need to buy a larger size when he is adult. Also, if your puppy is a chewer, take care that the plastic edges of the bed do not become dangerously sharp; if they do, I'm afraid you'll simply have to replace the bed.

When your English Springer is adult, he may be perfectly happy just to have a soft, comfy bed to lie on, but if this is your choice, make sure it is raised a couple of inches from the ground to avoid draughts.

It will not take long before your puppy views his crate as his own special den.

Dog crate

Some owners prefer their English Springer puppy to sleep in a crate rather than in a bed, but within the home it's just a matter of personal preference. It may be that you decide to keep a crate in the utility room or kitchen area and a softer bed in the sitting room.

Crates are not cages, as many non-dog owners tend to think; they are very practical pieces of dog equipment. They are useful both around the home and when travelling in the car, so I would certainly recommend that a puppy be crate-trained from an early age. Although a puppy may have plenty of freedom around the house, there may be times when you need to confine him, such as when you are doing the vacuuming or perhaps cooking. Consider, too, that if your dog ever has to go to the vet for observation or an operation, he will be confined to a box or a crate, so he will spend a much more relaxed time in the surgery if he is already crate-trained.

If sensibly trained with kindness, any dog will grow to look on his crate as his own special place and will go in there of his own accord if the door is left ajar, although he must have sufficient room to stand up and turn around comfortably. Crates are collapsible, so can be moved from one place to another, but many people like to get two, one for the home and one for the back of the car, for a crate is no mean weight to move about. An alternative is to have you car fitted with a crate, or maybe just a dog guard. The aim is not to allow your dog to bounce all over the seats and distract the driver, which could be very dangerous.

Bowls

You will need a bowl for your dog's crate, ideally one of the 'hook on' variety, or, for travelling, you may prefer one of the non-spill bowls. Around the home you will need a water bowl and food bowls, always sufficiently large for your dog to get his muzzle well inside so he can enjoy his meal.

I find stainless-steel bowls are best, as they can be kept clean very easily. Porcelain can chip and harbour germs, and plastic bowls are a definite 'no no'. Some people prefer to use heavy porcelain dishes for water, as they are less likely to be tipped over, but a lot depends on the delicacy of your Springer's drinking habits!

Your English Springer will travel safely in a car crate.

Food

If you have selected a genuinely good breeder who cares for the well-being of the puppies after they have moved to their new homes, you will be given careful guidance as to how to feed, with details of the make of food given, meal times and quantities. Ideally, these will have been printed out so no misunderstanding can arise. This way you can already have a suitable supply of food in stock before collecting your puppy. If you have difficulty in obtaining the same make, ask the breeder if you might have a small supply from her, so that you do not suddenly have to make the change to a new brand, which could upset your new puppy's tummy. (See page 59.)

Collar and lead

Puppy collars will not break the bank, so it will be both more comfortable and safer for your dog if you get him a few correctly sized collars while he is going through the growing stages. While he is still tiny and confined to your home, the collar should be light in weight, basically just to get him used to the feel of something around his neck. When he is taken out into the big, wide world beyond your gates, he will need something safe, with a secure catch that you must check regularly. The collar must be fitted so that it cannot slip over your Springer Spaniel's head if he pulls, particularly backwards, and not too tight to be uncomfortable. You should be able to slip two fingers underneath.

When it comes to the choice of fastening, a clip type (if it is a really good one) is probably better than a buckle, as it can always be released quickly if your dog gets into difficulty. Being a gundog, a youngster can easily get tangled up in something while out exploring.

The choice of lead is very much one of personal preference, and there is such a wide variety from which to choose these days. Chain leads can weigh heavy on the neck, and I have had a strong dog break a chain, for links can occasionally be weak. Nylon leads are strong and inexpensive, but always check the stitching. Perhaps the ultimate is a high-quality leather lead, which will be easy on your hand, though you will have to take care that a youngster doesn't chew through it. For the show ring, and also for gundog training, you will also require a slip lead.

Grooming equipment

It is possible to have an entire grooming bag jam-packed full of useful items, as there is so much variety of grooming equipment available, but you would be better advised just to have a few, carefully selected, high-quality items that will be of permanent use to you.

For an English Springer Spaniel, a soft bristle brush, a high-quality metal comb and a slicker brush are the essentials to keep the coat in good order. Nail clippers, a toothbrush and 'doggy' toothpaste should also be part of your kit, and you will need some good hairdressing scissors and a pair of thinning scissors, too.

Some owners also invest in a set of clippers when the dog is a bit older. Those that are easiest to use have no wire attached, but are electrically recharged on a base. You will need clipper blades and clipper oil, to keep them in good condition and to extend their life.

For further information on grooming, see Chapter Four.

Buy basic grooming equipment so your puppy can get used to being handled from an early age.

Toys

Every puppy needs toys and an English Springer Spaniel is no exception. He likes to retrieve, and toys and balls are good things with which he can begin to learn. You can also join in his fun with things like a Frisbee or a rubber ring, and an adult Springer can get a lot of pleasure out of a tug rope; this, though, should never be used before his jaw placement is fully formed, which is around 18 months of age.

Always check toys and other playthings regularly for damage, and if there is any sign of loose pieces, discretely remove them from his toy box when he is not looking!

The toys you buy must be tough enough to withstand the rigours of chewing,

FINDING A VET

You should try to sort out a suitable vet before your puppy arrives home, ideally one that has been recommended to you by someone you know and who has a dog that you are sure is well cared for. Do not be worried about paying a visit to various surgeries before you decide on the one you consider best. You can get a fair idea of what sort of support you can expect from the surgery by assessing the general atmosphere of the reception area, its staff and, of course, general cleanliness. Don't necessarily choose the one that is nearest to you, but, then again, your vet should never be located too far away in case you need him in an emergency. You may also wish to enquire whether the vet operates an appointment system, which avoids a long wait, or whether it's on a 'first come, first served' basis.

Your puppy will almost certainly need to go along to your vet for a check-up soon after he joins you, and to complete his course of vaccinations. You will probably also want to ask your vet to microchip your new family member, a very useful means of identification should he ever get lost.

BRINGING YOUR PUPPY HOME
When the day finally arrives and it is time to collect your puppy, make sure everything is prepared at home. For the journey you will need to take a drinking bowl and a supply of fresh water, preferably mineral water or boiled tap water if you are travelling any distance, as the breeder's supply and your own will be different and may upset his tummy. You will also need kitchen roll, some newspaper and a towel, for he may not travel well.

At last it is time to take your puppy home.

If he is still too young to be put on the ground in a public place because his course of vaccinations is incomplete, you will also have to make some provision for him to relieve himself en route if the journey is lengthy.

And, in the excitement of it all, don't forget to take from the breeder all the documentation you need. It is all too easy to give 100 per cent of your concentration to the puppy and to overlook something important.

Although you will very probably want your English Springer to become crate-trained for car travel, for this first journey I always feel the best idea is to have someone travel in the back seat, with the puppy securely tucked on their lap, on that all-important towel! He will probably never have travelled in a car before, certainly not without his littermates, so it is essential that he encounters as little stress as possible. Later you will be able to train him to travel in a crate, going on very short journeys, then gradually increasing their length.

MEETING THE FAMILY

When you arrive home, only the close members of your immediate family should be there to greet the puppy – and children must be warned in advance that they are not to get over-excited. It is best if they are all sitting down, preferably on the floor, so that puppy is not over-awed by too much activity going on around him. Don't allow the children to pick up the puppy at this stage; he will almost certainly be confused by his new surroundings and he could easily wriggle out of their arms and do himself damage.

The puppy's first port of call must be your garden so that he can relieve himself, preferably in a spot you have already designated as his toilet area. Be sure to stay with him all the while to give him confidence and to be sure he doesn't dash off somewhere out of sight. When he has had the opportunity for a drink and a meal, he must immediately be taken to your garden again, something that must become routine. Don't worry, by the way, if he doesn't eat much for the first 24 hours or so; he will eat when he is settled and is feeling hungry. However, you must check that he is drinking properly, as he must not be allowed

Supervise interactions between your puppy and children so that relations get off to a good start.

to dehydrate.

An English Springer Spaniel is easy to get along with, so should settle in fairly quickly and easily. When he has been with you for a few days and has got to know his immediate family members, you will be able to allow your wider circle of friends into the house to meet him. Try not to bombard him with too many new situations all at once and he will grow up to be a confident, well-adjusted, four-legged family member.

THE ANIMAL FAMILY

It may be that you have other pets living at home, so it will be necessary for the new arrival to meet them, too. After all, they are also part of your immediate family, and must certainly not be left out. If you have another dog waiting at home, be sure that you greet him first, before you make a fuss of the new puppy; it is very important that he is never allowed to feel left out, or he may come to resent the newcomer.

An older dog will usually take kindly to a young puppy and will not consider him a threat, but introductions must always be under close supervision. Never leave the two alone together until you are perfectly sure they are getting along well and have sorted out the pecking order.

At mealtimes, each dog must have his own bowl of food, though it is usual that they will share one communal water bowl. Again, supervise mealtimes so you are sure that the puppy's meal is not being sneakily gobbled up by a larger, hungry adult! Likewise, they must have separate beds, even though, in time, you may find them cuddled up together.

When introducing other family pets, you will need to use a lot of common sense, especially if the English Springer is from working lines with a stronger hunting instinct. Personally, I have always found that when a new dog is introduced to a family cat, the cat just keeps his distance for a while and they make their own introductions in due course. Others recommend crating the puppy and then letting the cat into the room to sniff at the crate. This may be a good idea in theory, but I feel the puppy should be crate-trained first, which would mean

In most cases, an adult will be happy to accept a puppy – but try not to interfere too much while they get to know each other.

Feeding

As mentioned on page 53, you should have received a diet sheet from the puppy's breeder and you should stick to this rigidly, at least for the first few days. You can then slowly adjust feeding times and introduce a revised diet if you decide to do so. However, any new food should be introduced little by little over a period of a few days, mixing the new kind of food with the old, in ever-increasing proportions.

It is also worth mentioning that if you have a cat in the house, you should be sure the puppy cannot reach his food. The smell of cat food is often appealing to dogs, but it is completely different in make-up and should not be given.

If the puppy who joins you is very young, he will probably still be on four meals a day, two meat-based and two cereal-based. If he is still drinking milk, take advice from the breeder, but I have always found that goats' milk is better suited to puppies. Before too long your puppy will tell you, in his own way, when he is ready to reduce to three meals a day, then eventually two. In adulthood you may decide to feed just one meal, with a light snack at the other end of the day, or to continue with two. A lot will depend on your English Springer's lifestyle, and you must always bear in mind that he should not be allowed to exercise strenuously for two hours either side of a heavy meal.

delaying the introduction for a few days.

Smaller household pets should be kept safely in their pens, just in case anything untoward happens – which it just might! In time, it may be possible to introduce them to each other without the little fellow coming to any harm, but only you will be able to decide if you are prepared to take the risk.

THE FIRST NIGHT

That first night in your home will be really strange for your puppy, and probably very distressing. Put yourself in his shoes: you are in a new place with people you have never seen before, and, worst of all, you have no siblings and mother to snuggle up to. It must be awful for him.

Nonetheless, you must start as

House-training

As soon as your puppy hears the household stir each morning, he will be up and about and will need to relieve himself immediately. It is no good creeping about quietly while you get showered and dressed; you can rest assured he will have heard you and you will go downstairs to find a puddle on the floor, and probably worse.

The first person to get up each morning simply must let your puppy outside. An English Springer is not a slow learner and will want to be clean. What you must not do is chastise him for doing his toilet in the wrong place, unless you actually catch him in the act. If you reprimand him even 30 seconds after he has performed his misdeed, he simply will not connect the two and will not understand what he has done wrong. Never, never rub your puppy's nose in what he has done; if he is caught in the act, a stern voice will be sufficient and then quickly show him to the door.

For the first few days, you may like to place newspaper down by his sleeping area, as he may not be able to hold his water all night long.

you mean to go on. If you take your puppy to bed with you that first night, however tempting it may be, he will expect to do the same every night for the rest of his life. He will grow larger pretty quickly, and you or your partner may prefer not to have a heavy Springer Spaniel sprawling all over the bed. I once made this mistake with a Deerhound, and you can imagine how much space she took up, especially with four long legs that thought nothing of stretching out with force when she was in a deep sleep. More than once I ended up on the floor!

Your young puppy's bed needs to be cosy, slightly raised from the ground to avoid draughts, and, of course, he must have access to a bowl of fresh water close by. For comfort you may like to provide him

Some people like to move the paper closer and closer to the door gradually, leaving a scent on the paper from the previous elimination, but this can be a bit hit and miss as to whether or not it works! Take it from me: the best method is to have a very short night's sleep yourself for a week or two!

Take your puppy out to the garden at regular intervals and he will soon learn what is required.

with a not-too-hot hot-water bottle, the sort that has a simple safe cover fitted over it. Another idea that puppies seem to like is to have a loud clock ticking in the room. Although he will be upset that first night, he will also be very, very tired, so should eventually fall soundly asleep. The first couple of nights will be the worst; from then on he should settle down comfortably without any further problems.

A RESCUED DOG

There can be several reasons for taking on a rescued dog. It may be that you feel you do not have the stamina to cope with the antics of a growing puppy; perhaps you are in the later years of life and are concerned that a young puppy of a reasonably long-lived breed might outlive you; or maybe you just feel that you would like to give a good home to an English Springer Spaniel that has fallen on hard times.

Whichever way you look at it, although an older dog may be easier in some ways, he can also be very demanding. Just like a puppy, the dog will find himself in an alien environment, with no idea when or where he should go to the toilet. Furthermore, he may also be restless for the first few nights

because he is missing his old home, however kind or otherwise that may have been.

If you have had a dog before, and therefore have some grooming items in stock, and perhaps even a bed and feeding bowls, there will still be an outlay of expense from the start. A rescued dog, understandably, will cost less than a show puppy, for example, but you will usually still be asked to pay a small fee, or a donation to the rescue society. You will also have veterinary bills to take into account, or perhaps insurance for your pet.

Former life

Before making the commitment, try to find out as much as you can about the dog's former circumstances and the reason why he went into rescue. This being a gundog, he may have been worked, so he may not suddenly accept a sedentary life if you have neither the time nor the energy to take him on long walks. There are many such factors to consider, just as seriously as you would for a puppy.

When your older dog arrives home, you should treat the situation in exactly the same way as you would if you were taking on a puppy. Everything must be ready

It takes time for a rescued dog to settle into a new home.

in advance of his arrival, and gates and boundaries should have been checked and double-checked for safety. Bear in mind that an older dog will have to adapt not only to a new place but also to new people, so keep visitors to a minimum until he is settled. When he is settled and happy in his new home, you will have the added reward of knowing that you will give him as good a 'second home' as he possibly could have, and he will undoubtedly thank you for it.

Caring For An English Spaniel Springer Spaniel

A n English Springer Spaniel is an easy dog to live with, which is why he is so popular, but you must never lose sight of the fact that he is a dog that was developed for work in the field, so he needs both physical and mental stimulation. Consider, too, that this is not a short-coated breed, so time must also be devoted to grooming. If he is to be a fit dog with a healthy coat, he will need to be fed a suitable diet.

CHOOSING A DIET

There is a saying that has long been popular among dog folk that 'a healthy coat comes from the inside out'. Of course, there is a lot more to keeping a coat in good condition than feeding, but if the food your dog eats is poor, no amount of work will get a coat in gleaming, tip-top condition.

There are numerous pre-prepared canine diets available these days, so most owners no longer concoct their own special recipes for their dogs, but some do. A dog's dietary requirements will change as he goes through the various stages of his life, and a working English Springer will require a very different diet from a show Springer, for a highly active dog who is out in the field for a large part of each day usually needs a higher protein content. From the other perspective, a less active dog generally requires less protein, so, as a dog slows down with age, his dietary requirements will alter.

The aim is to feed a diet that is suited to your dog's age and lifestyle.

NATURAL DIETS

If you prefer to feed your dog a natural diet, you may buy suitable meat from the butcher and mix it with dog meal or dog biscuits. He will also enjoy a few vegetables in his diet, but these should be fresh and lightly cooked. Mixing in old, stale vegetables is not a good idea. It is likely that if you are preparing such a diet yourself, you will also need to provide multi-vitamin tablets and probably some calcium, especially while your Springer is still growing. The motto is not to overdo them.

Whatever type of diet you feed your dog, I always feel that fresh carrots are a good addition. They are nice and crunchy, so help to keep the teeth clean, they don't add calories, and each carrot provides a dog with obvious pleasure. I have never yet had a dog who doesn't enjoy a raw carrot!

Commercial Diets

Commercial diets can be as simple as you like for you, the owner, but behind the scenes a great deal of careful and scientific research will have gone into deciding just the right quantity of each ingredient to make up a healthy, balanced diet. A commercial, tinned food will need to be mixed with a commercial biscuit, so you must be careful to read the instructions as to the proportions in which these should be given.

There are many complete diets on the shelves of pet stores and supermarkets, and even more at dog shows and other canine events. Clearly this is the easiest way to feed your English Springer. Strictly speaking, such diets should be fed exactly as they come out of the bag. For variety's sake, most manufacturers offer different flavours, so you might get a sack of rabbit flavour one week and perhaps lamb the next.

When feeding a diet prepared by a manufacturer, be very careful not to unbalance an otherwise well-balanced diet. Humans would not wish to eat the same food day in and day out, but dogs do not think along the same lines, just so long as they feel well fed and well nourished.

If a dog does become bored with his diet, this can be changed, but gradually. Change in a diet can easily cause loose bowel movements, so it is worth noting that live yoghurt or fresh curd is particularly useful to correct tummy upsets.

If you want to feed a truly natural diet, the BARF diet is the one to go for. BARF stands for Bones And Raw Food, or some say Biologically Appropriate Raw Food. Basically, dogs are fed the way that nature intended. In the wild, dogs lived off whole carcasses, which included meat, skin, internal organs and the contents of the stomach, which usually contained digested vegetation incorporating essential nutrients.

This is essentially a raw diet, as varied as possible, including lots of raw meaty bones. Foods include chicken wings, chicken necks, rabbit, oxtail, minced meats, lamb shanks, eggs and their shells, liver, heart, fish, yoghurt, vegetables, which have been pulped, and fruit. Garlic is also often included in the diet, but not all agree with this.

Some large dogs tend to swallow raw foods dangerously quickly, but if you know that your English Springer will enjoy a thorough chew and not gulp his food, then maybe this is the diet for you – and it will also pay dividends in the tooth-cleaning department.

FEEDING REGIME

English Springer Spaniel puppies are usually fed four meals a day, spaced out at fairly even intervals, until the age of about 12 weeks. But a puppy will need time to digest his food and relieve himself before bedding down for the night, so your schedule should take this into account. When a puppy moves to a new home, the breeder's routine should be adhered to as far as possible, but can be shifted slightly to suit your own family's routine over the first few days.

From about 12 weeks a puppy will usually be satisfied with only three meals a day, but these will be larger meals. Not only will there be fewer meals, but your puppy will be growing

When your puppy first arrives in his new home, he will need four meals a day.

Bones and Chews

Dog owners have different theories about whether or not to give bones; some prefer to avoid them completely, while others will only give them if raw. The most important thing is that they must not be of the kind that will splinter – cooked chicken and lamb bones being the worst. Even the biggest marrowbone will wear down small, so, before it gets to that stage, it should be discretely removed to avoid danger from choking.

An English Springer has a generous-sized mouth compared with many other dogs, so any chews given should be fairly substantial. This is because when a dog has been 'working' at a chew for a while, it will reduce substantially in size, creating the danger of swallowing and consequent choking. Unless your dog is well trained, don't try to take a chew out of your dog's mouth while he is enjoying it or he is likely to gulp it down whole. Instead, remove it without him noticing if you possibly can.

up fast so will need more food intake. By now, if you are feeding a complete food, you may have graduated to one suited to an older puppy. Not only will the make-up of the food have changed, but so will the size of the kibble.

By six months an English Springer should be down to two meals a day, and if you have not yet changed to what is generally called a 'Junior' diet,

now is the time to do so. Different breeding lines mature physically at different rates so the quantity of food a puppy eats at this age may vary. Your Springer should never be too 'skinny', but neither should he be obese; he should be well covered, but you should not be able to see his ribs. As an adult, you may decide to keep him on two meals a day, but could drop him down

Find a feeding regime that suits you and your dog.

to one, ideally with a light snack at the other end of the day.

Now is an appropriate time to remind you to keep your dog's worming schedule up to date; it will have been begun by the breeder and continued by you, but it is easy to let a worming regime get rather lax as your puppy grows into adulthood. If he has worms, the carefully planned feeding programme will have lost much of its effect. *For information on internal parasites, see Chapter Six.*

MEALTIMES

As already discussed, you will be able to adjust your puppy's mealtimes to fit in with your own family schedule, but what you should not do is suddenly change them. If, for example, the breeder fed the third meal of the day at 3 pm and it suits you better to move this back to 4 pm, do it over a two or three day period, shifting it by just 20 or 30 minutes a day.

SOCIAL DEVELOPMENT

The English Springer Spaniel is generally a very good-natured dog, so socialisation should not be too much of a problem. When you are satisfied

Avoiding

It is not only the amount of food your dog eats that will determine his weight, but also his height and overall size, bone structure and the amount of exercise he gets. Two English Springers of the same bodily make up, fed exactly the same amounts of food of the same quality, will differ in weight if one is a working dog while the other lazes around all day by the fireside.

Although the UK English Springer Breed Standard no longer includes a weight clause, it used to be 22.5 kgs (50 lbs) for dogs, with bitches a little lighter. The American Standard stipulates 50 pounds (22.5 kgs) for a 20-inch (51-cm) dog and 40 lbs (18 kgs) for a 19-inch (48-cm) bitch, which gives a pretty clear guide, though you should bear in mind that bone structure varies.

You will be able to get your dog weighed at the vet, but if you are strong enough, you can get on the

that your young puppy feels confident among close and extended family, you can widen his circle of friends. Obviously, his course of vaccinations must be complete before he can be taken out to a public place where he will meet other dogs and can socialise with them, too.

Some puppies can be chewers, especially when teething, so this should be taken into account. If you have any valuable pieces of furniture take sensible precautions and keep

them out of harm's way – just in case! Remember that any breed of dog, when bored, can become destructive, so always give your English Springer plenty to do to keep both mind and body active. From the early days of ownership you should teach him that he has to spend a little time alone; then, when you go out to the supermarket and the queue is longer than anticipated, he will not become anxious and consequently distressed by your absence.

Obesity

bathroom scales holding your dog, then weigh yourself alone and subtract one weight from the other.

If you find that your dog is putting on too much weight, take an honest look at the amount of treats he is getting – not just from you but from other members of the family. Treats are great as a training aid, but should be strictly limited, as they will certainly put on a few extra pounds.

A fit dog that is the correct weight will enjoy a better quality of life – and have an increased life expectancy.

KENNEL DOGS

I can fully appreciate that some English Springers are kept as kennel dogs, especially if they are worked, but my personal opinion is that no dog is happier than when living in the home. I know of kennels where dogs are put to bed at 5pm and they don't then get any human companionship until they are let out of their kennel at 7am or later. This is no life for a breed as sociable as the English Springer.

Even if your English Springer is worked and comes home tired out with muddy paws, surely there is some little uncarpeted area of your home in which he can rest comfortably and feel part of the human family?

GROOMING

Whatever kind of coat your dog has, some time must be devoted to care. The English Springer Spaniel falls pretty much into the middle of the road in this regard; he needs more

Holidays

Dogs are always a problem when it comes to holiday time. If your dog lives with you as a family companion, you will understandably be reluctant to put him into kennels while you are away, but there may be no alternative. If you do use a boarding kennel, preferably select one on personal recommendation, and make sure you go along to view before you make a booking. Discuss feeding and exercise at length before you book and be sure you are perfectly happy with the arrangements that are made. Also enquire at what time the dogs are put away for the night and at what time they rise. Kennels in the UK are not allowed to accept dogs unless they are fully vaccinated.

You may be lucky enough to have a family member or close friend to live in your home while you are away; this is ideal if the person is a dog lover and if you are sure that he or she will be able to cope with your English Springer. There are also professional dog sitters who will stay in your home, but the cost may well prove prohibitive, though if you have a number of dogs, it might work out less expensive than paying multiple kennel fees. Naturally you will require references if you are to allow a stranger into your home while you are not there.

Another possibility is that someone may look after your dog in their own home. This can be a good idea, but your dog will be in a strange place, so may not be quite as easy to handle as he usually is. You must also be certain that his 'temporary home' is absolutely dog-proof.

You may decide to take your dog on holiday with you in your own country, in which case you will need to check in advance that dogs are accepted at your chosen guesthouse or hotel. Most charge a small extra fee for a dog to stay in your room. It is also now possible

Holidays are even more fun if you can take your English Springer – but you may need to make alternative arrangements.

to travel to several countries abroad with your dog. Obviously, this needs very careful planning well in advance. If living in the UK, you will need to obtain a pet passport, which will not be issued until the vet has completed various vaccinations, including rabies for which a titre test is required to be sure the level of protection is sufficiently high.

The slicker brush is used to keep the feathering free from mats and tangles.

work than some breeds, but less than many others.

You should train your puppy to get used to a brush and comb from a very young age and then you will not encounter any problems in the future. Dogs learn to enjoy the grooming routine for it is a time when they can be totally at one with their owners. Grooming stimulates both the skin and hair follicles and so will ensure that your dog's natural oils feed the coat to give it a lovely sheen. Both you and your dog will feel very satisfied with the result at the end of each grooming session.

Use the slicker brush for the feathering on the ears, front legs, between the hind legs and under the body. Take the brush right through the coat, not just over the surface. The only time when you should need to use the slicker on the main body coat is when your Springer has rolled in something thoroughly obnoxious, which, being a Springer, he is almost certain to do from time to time, otherwise you will use a normal brush. After you have been through the feathering with your slicker brush, run though it again with a fine comb.

You may like to add a rubber

A rake helps to remove dead hairs, particularly when your Springer is shedding his coat.

'hound glove' to your grooming kit. This will fit over your hand like a glove, and, although not essential, can be very useful to remove dead coat.

Make sure you check all the awkward spots for the build-up of knots and mats, especially behind the ears and under the front legs. Remove thick hair from the inside of the ears to increase air circulation and, very carefully, trim the coat growing between the pads.

REGULAR CHECKS

Between full grooming sessions, you must always keep a check on your dog's coat and general well-being. It will become second nature to you to lift the ear-flaps and check the pads, especially after a run in the fields.

Teeth

Accustom your puppy to having his teeth inspected and lightly cleaned from a young age, but remember that, while he is teething, his gums will be very tender. Teeth cleaning should be a part of your normal grooming routine. You can use a small fingerbrush, made especially for the purpose, or a toothbrush (begin with a child's one) and special canine toothpaste.

Bathing

It is a general rule of thumb that an English Springer Spaniel should not be bathed more than twice each year, for bathing too frequently removes the natural oils from the coat. Some owners do, however, bathe their dogs more regularly than that. Regular grooming will keep the coat fairly clean, but a thorough bath once in a while will freshen it up enormously.

Always use a dog shampoo, not a human one; a medicated shampoo that acts as an insecticide is a good choice. Follow the manufacturer's instructions if it needs to be diluted. If you wish, you may use a special rubber brush to get right though the coat, holding this in the palm of your hand. Make sure the water is not too hot, so test it on the back of your hand before you start.

Rinse the coat out thoroughly, until the water runs clear and the hair is 'squeaky clean'. Squeeze out any excess water before lifting your dog carefully out of the bath, and be prepared for him to have a good shake. Then towel dry him as much you can and finish off with a hairdryer.

If you brush your dog's teeth regularly, you should avoid the need to have his teeth scaled by a vet, though this is something that professional breeders frequently do themselves. Diet will also play a large part in keeping your English Springer's teeth clean.

Ears

Because of the length and positioning of an English Springer Spaniel's ears, they are more prone to trouble than those of a dog that has upright, open ears. Added to this, the Springer is a gundog that loves to forage in the fields where it

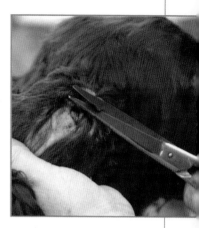

Regular teeth cleaning will help to prevent the build-up of tartar.

Wipe the ears clean with cotton-wool – but do not probe into the ear canal.

Hair that grows on the inside of the ear should be trimmed.

is all too easy for dirt and grass seeds to find their way into the ear – and grass seeds have a nasty habit of finding their way into the ear canal. It is for these reasons that ear care for this breed is of the utmost importance.

Check the ears every day and keep the hair inside the ear trimmed short. Use special ear wipes to keep the ears clean, but don't poke too deeply inside the ear or you can very easily cause harm. Signs of ear infection are when your dog shakes his head, scratches very regularly behind the ear or leans his head on one side. He may even rub his ear along the ground to try to relieve the discomfort; this is not the same as when he decides to rub himself in

something particularly smelly, such as fox poo! Frequently, there will be an odour and brown discharge with an ear infection. Urgent veterinary attention should always be sought, for the sooner the matter is dealt with, the sooner your dog will be out of pain.

Nails

You should begin clipping your English Springer's nails while he is still young so that he becomes accustomed to the procedure and accepts it readily. There is nothing worse than a dog who hates having his nails clipped, for there is always the fear that if he wriggles, you may make a mistake and cut the quick, causing the nail to bleed.

Hold him steady and talk to him quietly but firmly, so that he knows who has the upper hand. Always cut off a very thin slither of nail at a time; it is far better to take off a small amount of nail regularly, for the quick will recede each time, avoiding the danger of bleeding.

EXERCISING YOUR ENGLISH SPRINGER SPANIEL

As mentioned earlier, you should not exercise your puppy a great deal until he is fully matured, but when he is, his energy will know no bounds. By this time you should have trained him to come back to your recall, so

If properly trained, your English Springer will tolerate nail-clipping without making a fuss.

that he can be safely let off the lead, which will mean that you are walking far fewer miles than your dog!

Springers are also good swimmers, as they were bred to retrieve from water, and swimming is an excellent form of exercise. However, before allowing your dog in water, you must be certain that conditions are absolutely safe.

FUN AND GAMES

Whatever their age, Springer Spaniels love games for they exercise the body as well as the mind. Ball games are always enjoyable, but make sure the ball is not so small that it could be swallowed. Always check that squeaky toys are not at risk of losing their squeaks and that those that contain stuffing are not disembowelled, for both are dangerous if swallowed.

Toys of the 'ragger' variety can be entertaining, especially if you have more than one dog; it can be great fun watching them work out who will be the winner in the end!

CLEAN UP!

If you own a dog, it is your responsibility to clean up after him, both in a public place and at home, where your garden and patio or yard must also be kept scrupulously clean. Always carry a couple of poo bags

EXERCISING YOUR ENGLISH SPRINGER

English Springers have a natural love of swimming and playing in water.

Regulate exercise according to your dog's age and lifestyle.

A game of retrieve is an added bonus.

when out with your dog, and, when used, I am afraid you'll just have to hang on to them until you locate a suitable receptacle. Remember that nothing annoys the public more than watching a dog soil the pavement or playground while the owner or handler walks on nonchalantly. Make sure that owner isn't you!

PAIN THRESHOLD

Different dogs have different levels of pain threshold, so you should always keep in your mind that even though your English Springer may be injured, he may just work through his pain. At any sign of strain or limping, stop exercising him at once, let him rest, and, if necessary, seek a veterinary opinion.

If circumstances change, be sensitive to your Springer's needs.

CHANGING CIRCUMSTANCES

Your English Springer Spaniel will hopefully live 11 years or more, during which time changes may happen in your life, and indeed within your family. When changes come about, always make certain that your dog does not feel that his nose has been pushed out. If you have a new family member, such as a baby or an elderly relative, make introductions carefully and all should run smoothly, thanks in no small part to this breed's easy-going personality.

Children may also have grown up and moved away from home, so remember that it will not only be you who is missing them, but also their canine friend. Another change that might come about is a move of house, perhaps even to another part of the country; maybe your family will even split up. By now your dog will know you and hopefully respond to your commands, but exercise caution in the early days in case he is confused and tries to return to his old home.

Be aware of the changing needs of your English Springer as he gets older.

even more so as your dog gets older.

His requirement for food intake will also change with age. As he becomes less active, he will need slightly less food, but take care that if he still has an enthusiastic appetite he does not over-eat and therefore become obese. By now, if you are feeding a complete diet you may well have changed to the 'senior' variety, and you will almost certainly find your dog prefers to have two, or even three, smaller meals each day, rather than one large one.

If you are at all worried about your old boy's health, get in touch with your vet immediately. Often a dog can be given medication that will ease his pain and may prolong his life, providing his ailment has been attended to at a relatively early stage in its development.

THE OLDER ENGLISH SPRINGER

As your beloved English Springer gets older he will gradually slow down, so don't ever force him to do more than he feels he can cope with. When he goes out for walks, or perhaps a run in the field, make sure he is always dried down thoroughly upon returning home to prevent him from developing achy joints. This is always advisable, but

LETTING GO

Sadly, the time will eventually come when you have to part with your old friend, who has given you so many years of companionship and enjoyment. If you are lucky, he will go peacefully in his sleep, saving you the agony of making that dreaded decision about whether or not the time has come to have him put to sleep by the vet. But in the majority of cases, I am afraid the decision will rest with you.

Because you have grown to know your dog over the years, you will also know whether or not his quality of life has diminished so much that he can no longer obtain any enjoyment at all from it, or if his pain cannot be relieved.

It will take time, but after the pain of losing your English Springer, you will be able to look back on all the happy times you spent together.

When the time does come, the end is usually peaceful and almost imperceptible. Stay with your dog until it is over, all the while talking to him, ideally with your hand resting on his body to give him comfort. Try not to let him know how upset you are, for this will not help him – there will be plenty of time for tears after he has gone.

You might wish to bury your English Springer in the garden or perhaps arrange an individual cremation, which can be organised by your vet. This will not be cheap, but surely your pet deserves this final gesture, and then you may bury his ashes where you wish and remember all the happiness you shared together each time you pass the spot.

Educating Your English Spaniel Springer

An English Springer Spaniel can be a remarkable companion, obedient, energetic, intelligent and thoroughly devoted to his owner. But no dog, however suitable the breed, comes 'ready trained'. An English Springer, just like any other breed, needs work and it is you, the owner, who must be prepared to do that. The effort you put in will be well rewarded, but you must work hard at it, and not give up along the way.

EARLY SOCIALISATION

We have already discussed how, when your puppy arrives home, he should only be introduced to the close members of your family. He will need to learn who is who and to understand his own role within his family. It is during these early few days that he will learn to cope with the situations that life will throw at him as he grows older.

One of the reasons why you must be very careful from whom you buy your puppy is that the ages of 4-10 weeks are very important in early socialisation. During the first 10 days, when his eyes are still not open, his main stimuli are the warmth and movement of his dam and littermates. Some people prefer not to handle newborn puppies very much, but provided the dam is not disturbed by it, I always do, though I would always handle them near their dam, so she does not get distressed. In this way, even before they have their eyes open, the puppies start to

become familiar with me and with my scent. They will also get used to me checking them over, feeling their bodies to assess their construction, at which point I will take note of anything that may appear to be going wrong with their development. I will pick up their feet to trim their tiny toenails, not only to get them used to having their nails attended to but also to save their dam from discomfort, as sharp nails pounding into a dam's teats must be so painful. All this hands-on contact is, I feel, good for puppies and will help them to adjust to other people handling them later in life.

As the puppies grow older, they will have more and more contact with people, including children, so they will grow up to be well-adjusted adults. Even before they leave for their new homes, they need to become accustomed to the kind of sounds they will hear every day– taps running, kettles boiling and the vacuum, something many dogs do

A puppy has a lot to learn when he first arrives in his new home.

A well-socialised English Springer will take all new experiences in his stride.

not take to kindly, probably because the sound moves around the house. Washing machines make a goodly noise too, especially when they are on spin, as indeed does the television and the radio. In fact, in boarding kennels a radio is often left on for the dogs, even through the night, and this can also be useful in the home if the owner has to go out for two or three hours. Choose a programme with a mixture of talking and music – in Britain, I always feel that Radio 2 is the best bet!

SOCIALISING WITH OTHER DOGS

Because of their easy-going nature, English Springers usually get along well with other dogs, whatever their size. I would always caution owners of small dogs to take care when their pets are around larger dogs that are essentially working dogs, but if introduced properly under supervision, there is usually no problem. The problems can occur when a dog sights a small bundle of fluff some distance away and rushes off to investigate.

Dogs work in packs so when there is more than a single dog, they will sort out the hierarchy between themselves. If several dogs are living together, the order of hierarchy may change over the years as a dominant dog grows older and less sprightly, allowing a younger one to take over. This is not usually a problem with English Springers, for they are a peaceable sort of a crowd, but you should always keep in mind that, as their owner, they should see you as the most dominant member of their little tribe.

You will have to be more careful about temperament around the times of a bitch's season when the girls can be a little skittish, and, of course, the men-folk want the ladies, so can be more antagonistic among themselves.

If you have an only dog and want to introduce him to others, it can be a good idea to go along to a ringcraft or obedience class with your youngster to let him meet other dogs in a controlled environment. If you are hoping to show your English Springer, a ringcraft class is the one you will need, but if you have a dog you hope to work or just keep as a family pet, obedience classes would be more suitable.

At both of these types of training class your dog will have to learn manners and to interact sociably when in close contact with other dogs; and the dogs he will meet are likely to come in all shapes and sizes, which can only be a good thing. He will also get more exposure to people, who will handle and fuss him, building on his social skills. When

If you put in time training your English Springer, he will be happy to accept his place in the family pack.

your young English Springer is behaving well with other dogs, remember to give him plenty of praise, so he knows you are pleased with his behaviour. When your puppy meets another potential canine friend, the meeting should be on reasonably neutral territory not, for example, a first meeting at the other dog's bed which is full of his toys and a chew – that would just be asking for trouble. Your English Springer may be pretty laid back, but the other fellow may think differently!

On-going Socialisation

Once you feel that your puppy is sufficiently well socialised, don't just forget about it and deprive him of chances to meet other dogs and people. Continue to take him along to his training classes, even if you decide to drop down the frequency. You should also take him on a lead walk around your local area; you are sure to come across people you want to chat to and, with luck, they will also be walking their dogs.

TRAINING THE ENGLISH SPRINGER SPANIEL

As you are the main food provider, your dog will automatically see you as the leader of his pack, even if, in his eyes, you are only a pack of two. Given your standing in the order of things, you will also have to gain his respect as the decision maker. You will need to be a good leader, for it is only if you are not that problems will start to arise.

You must start as you mean to go on so that your Springer is not allowed to get the upper hand before you have even commenced his training. You must be very clear in your instructions; don't allow him to do one thing one day and not the next or he simply will not know what is right and what is wrong.

If you are to be a good leader, you must also get your timing right. Praise him when he is good and reprimand him when he is bad, but instantly. If you tell him he has done something wrong even a few seconds after the misdeed, he simply will not comprehend the connection. As you get to know your dog better, you will learn to understand his body language and even though he does not have the power of speech, you will have a pretty good idea of what he is trying to say. Just as you read his body language, he will learn to read yours. English Springers also seem to have the ability to read your thoughts, even before you have begun to express them. He will also listen and respond to your tone of voice, so don't be afraid to exaggerate your 'happy voice', and, when you want him to know that he has displeased you, make it clear by your stern tone.

You will need to be consistent in your training in terms of regularity too, including when he is older, for there may come a time when he decides to challenge you. You should train him to allow you to walk though a door before he does, never to leap out of a car door when it is opened (only upon command), and repeatedly get him to give up his toys when you request them. To do this you will probably have to offer to exchange them with him for something he also likes, but this is a very important lesson for all dogs, especially a gundog.

Training benefits

Training your dog will have important benefits for future harmony. It will emphasise your role as the pack leader, clearly defining that you are the boss and that your dog is lower down the 'pecking order'. Training will also enable you to build a closer bond with your dog and you will be able to stimulate his mind so that he is always alert and listening to your every command.

Collar and lead training

Introduce your puppy to a soft, comfortable collar within a couple of days of him settling into your home, for this will get him used to the fact that he has something around his neck. To begin with, just leave it on for a few minutes at a time, always

The aim is for your English Springer to walk on a loose lead – neither pulling ahead nor lagging behind.

Verbal Communication

Firstly, you must keep in mind that your English Springer should learn only one word for each action, otherwise he will be confused. The most usual words to teach him are: 'Come', 'Sit', 'Down', 'Stay', 'No', 'Leave' and 'Wait'.

Other words will certainly creep into your mutual vocabulary over time. 'Off' can be used, for example, when he has jumped on the furniture, probably with muddy feet. 'Toilet' is a useful word to teach – this can come in particularly handy when your dog is out in a strange environment and doesn't seem to know where he should do a poo. If your dog is pulling on the lead, 'Steady' will come in handy to slow him down, and, at the end of the day, 'Bed' can be used to indicate that it is time now to rest.

If you have more than one dog, you should use the dog's name before the command – otherwise, your entire canine tribe will respond! The name you use for your dog should be a fairly short one that your dog can recognise easily.

staying with him, and you will find that, within a day or two, he will be happy to keep it on all the while.

When you are happy that he is totally comfortable wearing a collar, you should attach a lightweight lead, encourage your puppy to come toward you and make a big fuss of him. By doing this, he will associate you with the lead. Since he will like to be with you, this will make the lead acceptable to him.

Soon enough you will be able to take him on short walks, initially in

Make yourself sound exciting so your English Springer wants to come to you.

your garden where he already feels safe and secure. At first he may be reluctant to come when pulled gently; I always allow my dogs to lead me for the first two or three times so they get used to the fact that I am attached to the other end. Soon the tables can be turned so that I am 100 per cent in control. As with any other training session, always end on a high note, praising your dog for something he has done well.

The 'Come' and 'Sit' commands

'Come' is a word that will be easily learned by your English Springer Spaniel puppy, as this is something he will have heard from the very beginning of his time with you when you have called him to you. He will have enjoyed coming to you for fuss and attention, and this is the word you will have used when you first introduced his puppy lead. But 'Come' can now be combined with other commands; you can teach him to 'Sit' or 'Stay' and then come back to you.

Teaching 'Sit' is also not too difficult and is easier with a dog the size of an English Springer than with a very small dog. Hold a treat just above your dog's nose, and, when he looks up at the treat, he will very probably automatically end up in the sit position. If he does not, press his rear end gently down into the sitting position, giving the command "Sit". You can practise the sit command not only with treats but also at mealtimes, holding the bowl up until your dog sits.

Teaching your dog to go into the 'Down' position is one of the most useful of all the training exercises.

Teaching 'Down' and 'Stay'

Teaching 'Down' is harder than 'Sit', but it should be taught, as this can be very useful. Instruction can commence either when the dog is standing or sitting but, in this instance, you will hold a treat below your dog's nose and slowly lower it to the ground. Your Springer's nose will follow it, at first lowering his forequarters and then his hindquarters, too. If you need to, you can apply gentle pressure on his shoulders to get him into the position you require. Take care that your dog cannot get the treat until he is completely in the 'Down' position, so grip your hand tightly around the treat. Use the verbal command as your dog is going down.

To begin with, you will have to give the treat to your dog straight away, but each time you do the exercise, make him wait a little longer so that he learns to stay in this position.

The 'Stay' command will follow on naturally from 'Sit' and 'Down'. Take a couple of steps backward, indicating with the flat palm of your hand towards him that he must stay. Then call him to you immediately and give him praise, before he has had time to think about why you have left him. Only extend the distance between you and your dog when you feel confident that he has mastered the 'Stay' command at the distance you have already practised.

Teaching 'No' and 'Leave'

The tone of your voice and your body language are important factors when

Teach your English Springer to 'Wait' until he receives the next command.

teaching the words 'No' and 'Leave'. 'No' should be used to tell him not to do something; it is not a word that should be over-used. 'Leave' can be used more frequently, such as when you want your dog to drop a toy or a bone. For neither of these commands should your dog expect to receive a treat, but, to begin with, you will have to give him 'a treat' in the form of plentiful praise, until he has learned to respond to these words as soon as they are uttered.

Teaching 'Wait'

'Wait' is another useful command to teach your English Springer, as it can be used for a variety of things, such as when you want him to wait while you open the gate, or to pause before crossing a road, giving you time to check that the way is clear. Your dog will soon learn that after hearing the word 'Wait', and after he has, of course, waited, something will follow and that will be sufficient impetus for him to learn.

OPPORTUNITIES FOR ENGLISH SPRINGERS

The English Springer Spaniel is a wonderful dog, both elegant and intelligent and with a great personality to boot. This makes him suitable for all sorts of situations and means that you can take part in many different activities with your dog.

Exhibiting in the show ring

Showing an English Springer Spaniel can be lots of fun and will enable you

The Ideal English Springer Spaniel Owner

- As a good English Springer Spaniel owner, you will be a loving, caring person, who is always consistent when giving commands. Your tone of voice will be stern when needed, but you will never be overtly angry or abusive towards your dog; if you were, he would lose his respect for you.
- When he has been good you will reward him with plenty of praise, a very important part of training that must never be overlooked.
- You will never forget to end your training session on a positive note, so that both he and you are pleased with what has been achieved and will look forward to the next learning opportunity.

The Springer is an intelligent, responsive dog, so make training sessions fun and rewarding for both of you.

to make a whole new circle of friends if you have not been involved in the show world before. But this is a competitive breed and competition is fierce; to win well you will need a high-quality dog that is presented to perfection and shown by an enthusiastic, capable handler.

There are various levels of shows, and at some you will stand more chance of going home with a red 'first prize' card. There are Companion Shows, which are always run for a charitable cause and can make for an enjoyable day out. Entries are taken on the day and there are no breed-specific classes.

Basically, they are a just a bit of fun, but good fun at that!

For the serious show-goer, you will want to consider entering Open or Championship Shows, and if this is your first show dog, I would strongly recommend that you enter a few Open Shows first of all to see how you and your dog get along.

At an Open Show you will pick up tips from other exhibitors and you must use your eyes carefully to be sure that you are showing and presenting your dog correctly, for if not, you will stand no chance of having your dog placed at a subsequent Championship event.

At the top level competition in the show ring is intense.

Field Trials will test an English Springer's natural hunting and retrieving abilities.

Both Open and Championship Shows must be entered in advance, but Championship Shows cost substantially more and usually have a greater selection of breed classes. Other shows at these levels are Breed Shows run by English Springer Spaniel clubs; these are always enjoyable and here you will learn a great deal from many enthusiastic breeders and exhibitors who have gone along to show their dogs.

You will be able to find details of all shows in the canine press, and many societies now also post details on the internet, from which you can download an application form.

Hopefully, before you go to your first show you will have done some ringcraft training with your dog, and if your English Springer Spaniel has turned out to be as well constructed as you and his breeder had hoped, you will undoubtedly have some very enjoyable times ahead.

Field Trials

In Field Trials it is an English Springer Spaniel's natural working ability that is put to the test, and if this is your goal, you should have purchased your puppy from working stock.

Dogs train in a natural environment and are required to retrieve shot game from different kinds of terrain, such as swamps and land with thick undergrowth. They also have to retrieve from water. In addition to retrieving game they have seen fall, they are also trained to find shot game that they have not seen fall.

English Springers that take part in Field Trials are judged on their natural gaming abilities, work in the shooting field, and response to their handler; they are required to be not only steady, but also obedient.

If you and your English Springer work well together, you may even aim for the title of Field Trial Champion, but you could also aim for the Gundog Working Certificate, which is also a very highly deserved achievement. Although show and working English Springers rarely combine their activities, if a Show Champion also gains a Working Certificate, he can become a full Champion; but full Champions are few and far between.

Working Trials

Working Trials comprise three main components: control, in which dog and handler complete obedience exercises; agility, negotiating a hurdle, long jump and a 6 ft (1.83 m) upright scale; and also nosework, which involves following a track that has been laid over a set course. For

The Kennel Club Good Citizen Scheme

This scheme is run by the Kennel Club and has now been taken up by the kennel clubs of some overseas countries, too. There is a Puppy Assessment Foundation for youngsters, leading to the Bronze, Silver and Gold Awards, increasing in complexity.

The exercises are fairly basic, but important if your English Springer Spaniel is to be a polite member of the community.

The English Springer is an enthusiastic competitor in agility.

Working Trials you will need to seek out a specialist club or a specialist trainer.

Agility

Agility is a fun sport and a challenging one, too! For this you will need a certain degree of stamina yourself for you will have to run round the agility course with your Springer, though you will not have to jump the jumps!

Your dog will need to be fit and certainly not overweight, for he will have to jump upright hurdles and also do long jumps, as well as weaves, going over an A-frame, a dog walk and negotiating a see-saw. He will also have to jump through tyres and go through tunnels, so he will certainly have his work cut out.

To compete, a dog must be a minimum of 18 months old, though training may begin at 12 months. Faults are awarded as the dog goes round the course, the aim being to complete the course without faults and in the fastest time. All in all, it's enormous fun for a fit English Springer.

A Hearing Dog can transform the life of a deaf person.

English Springers helping others

Finally, the English Springer Spaniel is such a well-loved dog that he makes a very good candidate for therapy work. There are now several charities for various types of therapy work in which dogs can assist people in less fortunate circumstances than ourselves.

Dogs can be of great assistance to those who are deaf, blind or physically disabled, and, through an organisation such as Pat Dogs in the UK, they can visit homes for the terminally ill, or care homes where many residents have loved dogs all their lives but have sadly found themselves in a position whereby they can no longer own a dog. To see the expression on such people's faces when they hug and caress your English Springer Spaniel will reward all the effort you have put into his training.

Health Care For The English Springer Spaniel

O nce you have decided on your veterinary practice, it is important to take your new English Springer Spaniel for a health check as soon as possible. This first examination can be the beginning of a long and happy relationship between your Springer Spaniel and his veterinary surgeon, and it is a good idea for your vet to get to know him from an early age.

Regular 'weigh-ins' and visits to the surgery to pick up medication for worming and treatment of fleas will accustom him to visiting the vet with no adverse experiences. A few dog treats go a long way in making the consulting room a pleasant place! It is also a good idea for you to mimic a clinical examination at home so your Springer is used to having his ears, eyes, mouth and body inspected.

VACCINATION

Vaccination is vital to prevent and control some of the severe viral and bacterial diseases that can be fatal to dogs. Vaccines work by stimulating the body's natural immune response to provide protection should your dog ever be exposed to the disease. This protection is continued each year by annual booster vaccinations. It is important to remember that your Springer Spaniel should be as fit and healthy as possible to help the vaccine work fully.

Puppies obtain antibodies from their mother's colostrum (first milk), providing immunity to disease for the first few weeks of life. The level of immunity depends on the number of antibodies absorbed from the colostrum and how well the mother is protected from certain diseases. Over a period of time, differing for each puppy, these antibodies decrease, and, from six weeks of age, a puppy will need his first vaccination. The initial vaccination course contains at least two injections, the second vaccination being given after 10 weeks of age. Contact with unvaccinated dogs or at-risk areas should be avoided until full immunity is established.

The diseases protected against by standard vaccination protocols are briefly outlined here, but if your Springer Spaniel is diagnosed with any of the following, he should be kept away from other dogs to prevent the spread of infection.

- **Distemper:** Caused by the canine distemper virus (CDV).
- **Infectious canine hepatitis:** Caused by canine adenovirus-1 (CAV-1).
- **Parvovirus:** Caused by canine parvovirus (CPV) that can survive for months to years in the environment.
- **Leptospirosis:** Caused by two main strains of spirochaete bacteria, *Lepstospira icterohaemorrhagiae* (affects the liver) and *L. canicola* (affects the kidneys).
- **Kennel cough:** Caused by multiple viral and bacterial agents and highly infectious.
- **Herpes:** Caused by the canine herpes virus (CHV).

PARASITES

English Springers are outgoing and active working dogs with an interest – and a nose – in everything! This will result in contact with parasites, both internal and external, but is not necessarily a serious issue if they are adequately controlled. There are several types of worm, the most common being the roundworm. Most puppies are born with infection; in adults, infection often occurs from eating infected faeces or meat or via an intermediate host.

Treatment in most cases requires worming medication to remove the infection and ongoing preventative medication to prevent build-up. All worming medication should be discussed with your veterinary surgeon for timing, frequency and the choice of preparation.

Strict hygiene, especially with faeces, should always be observed. When out walking your dog, faeces should be removed from public places with a bag and many parks now provide disposal bins specifically for this purpose. This, as well as enabling walking without stepping into unpleasant matter, helps reduce the infection of other dogs and in some cases humans.

Roundworms

Toxocara canis: This is a large, round, white worm found in the small intestine. Signs of infection are a pot-belly, occasional diarrhoea or vomiting, poor growth, lethargy, coughing, pneumonia, nasal discharge and even death in young pups with very heavy infections. The regular worming of pups and mother during the early periods of the puppies' lives will prevent severe

Puppies should be routinely treated for roundworm.

infections. Adult dogs should be treated every three to six months throughout their lives. It is important to note that, although unlikely, this worm can infect humans. It is seen most commonly in children who have had close contact with household pets or areas contaminated with dog faeces, potentially resulting in liver damage or blindness.

Tapeworms

Dipylidium caninum:

This is the most common of the tapeworm species in the UK. Infection occurs via ingestion of fleas and lice carrying the intermediate lifestage of the worm. The adult worms live in the small intestine and release proglottids (mobile segments containing the eggs) into the faeces. The adults rarely cause clinical disease, although irritation of the anus may be seen as the proglottids emerge. Treatment and control are integral, with insecticide treatment preventing the completion of the lifecycle, while regular worming medication removes the adult worms.

Spot-on treatment is an effective preventative for external parasites.

Fleas

Ctenocephalides canis and C. felis (more common): When the flea bites, it causes irritation to the skin, which results in itching and inflammation. Regular flea insecticide treatment is required on the dog and good hygiene and aerosol treatment in the environment to help break the reproductive cycle and reduce numbers.

Ticks

The common types of tick found on dogs in the UK are the *Ixodes ricinus*

Mites

Otodectes cyanotic: This mite is found in the external ear canal and causes a brown, waxy discharge, resulting in head shaking, discomfort and pruritis. It can be transmitted by close contact. Infection can be cleared by cleaning the ear canal and applying medicated drops.

Cheyletiella yasguri: This mite is visible with the naked eye and is often referred to as 'walking dandruff'. Treatment is available and effective. Care must be taken, as this parasite is zoonotic (transferable to humans).

(sheep tick) and the *I. hexagonus* (hedgehog tick). They are blood-sucking parasites that can transmit diseases such as Lyme disease (to both dogs and humans) and Erlichiosis. Bean shaped, they vary in size from 2-10 mms and are most commonly found on dogs in spring and autumn.

Ticks can be removed using a tick removal tool, engaging the hook under the tick and flat to the skin of the dog and twisting the body until the tick comes out. Take care not to squeeze the body or leave the mouthparts in the skin, as infection can occur.

Ringworm/Dermatophytosis

Microsporum canis is responsible for the majority of ringworm cases with *Trichophyton mentagrophytes* and *Microsporum gypseum* also seen. Typically, circular lesions are present with skin scaling and hair loss noted. Topical treatment is used; if infection is severe, antibiotics may also be needed.

Demodex canis: This cigar-shaped burrowing mite is found in small numbers on healthy dogs, but disease can occur if the immune system is compromised. Transmission occurs between mother and pups while feeding, and infection is often seen in young dogs with scaling, hair loss, pustules and skin infections especially around the face. Occasionally the feet may be affected. Treatment involves repeated applications of topical medication and occasionally antibiotics.

Sarcoptes scabiei: This highly contagious burrowing mite causes intense itching around the ears, muzzle, face and elbows and, if severe, all over the body. Clinical signs involve pustules, crust formation, alopecia and there may be self-trauma from itching. Treatment requires repeated bathing with a medicated shampoo, with isolation until eliminated to prevent transmission.

A-Z OF COMMON AILMENTS

Anal gland disorders

Anal glands are small sacs that empty into the anus when defecation occurs. They produce a dark-brown, pungent liquid, which is used by dogs to mark their territory. Occasionally they may become blocked or impacted, resulting in irritation and causing your Springer Spaniel to drag his bottom along the floor (scooting), have problems toileting, or nibble around the tail area.

At this point the glands can be manually expressed to clear the blockage. If the blockage is not cleared, then infection may occur and form an abscess within the gland. This will need veterinary attention.

Factors that may play a part in causing impaction are diarrhoea, soft faeces and obesity. English Springers can suffer from anal gland problems and persistent recurrence may eventually require surgery to remove the affected gland completely.

Dental problems

Periodontal disease is the most common oral disease in dogs, and English Springers are no exception. Tartar can be seen as young as nine months of age and is normally first noticed on the upper back teeth, spreading and getting worse over time. Your dog's teeth should be examined regularly to assess the level of disease and to decide whether treatment is necessary.

Minimal deposit on the teeth can be controlled with a healthy diet, tooth brushing and dental chews. Tooth brushing should be taught at an early age – prevention is better than cure!

Once tartar has formed, this cannot be removed by brushing and will only become worse with time. At this point, an anaesthetic may be needed to remove the tartar manually. The condition of the teeth beneath the tartar determines whether or not they need extracting. After dentistry, it is very important to maintain dental health and it may be advisable to alter the diet to encompass your dog's dental requirements.

Ear infections

Infection can occur commonly in the outer ear (**otitis externa**), resulting in a brown, waxy discharge, often accompanied with a characteristic smell and reddening of the skin. This will cause your dog to shake his head or scratch at his ears in response to the irritation. If the infection spreads deeper into the middle ear (**otitis media**) or inner ear (**otitis interna**) then this may cause neurological signs, such as lack of co-ordination, imbalance, circling or a head tilt.

English Springers can be susceptible to ear infections and irritations due to their long pinnae, narrowing of the ear canal in some dogs and their love of water. Regular grooming and trimming of the hair

You will need to keep a constant check on your English Springer's ears.

inside the ear flap will help to maintain healthy ears. Occasionally, foreign bodies (e.g. grass seeds) can enter the ear canal and remain there. Ear mites (see page 104) cause irritation and wax production. Bacteria and yeasts can enter the ear and infection becomes apparent if uncontrolled growth occurs.

Treatment involves clearing any infection and removing excess wax. There are many topical preparations available, but if infection is severe or non-responsive, investigation under anaesthetic may be required to flush the ear canal. If left untreated, the

Endocrine disorders

The endocrine system influences all body functions based on glands and the hormones they produce.

Hypothyroidism: This is a common endocrine disease where there is an underproduction of thyroxine (hormone controlling the metabolic rate of the body) from the thyroid gland. Generally seen in middle-aged dogs of larger breeds, the Springer Spaniel is not seen to be at an increased risk. The low levels result in weakness, lethargy, reduced body temperature, slow heart rate, hair loss, weight gain and skin problems. Treatment, often successful, is in the form of an oral synthetic hormone.

ear may become impacted, the skin may become thickened from chronic inflammation, and ultimately surgery may be the only option.

Eye disorders

Eyelids: The eyelids cover and protect the delicate structures of the eye and ensure that the outer surface remains clean and lubricated. English Springer Spaniels may suffer from both **entropion** (eyelids turning inwards) and **ectropion** (the eyelids droop outwards), which may result in

inflammation and infection. Small, wart-like growths on the lids may occur, which is not usually a problem unless they grow large or touch the cornea and cause trauma.

Lens: The lens is found behind the pupil and focuses light rays so that objects can be seen clearly. **Cataracts** are an opacification (blue-whitening) of the lens, progressively resulting in impaired vision, not to be confused with **nuclear sclerosis** (grey-blue haze) which occurs in older animals

Diabetes mellitus (DM): This is one of the most common endocrine disorders encountered, most often seen in middle-aged, overweight dogs. Glucose is absorbed by cells in the presence of insulin, and is the energy source for cell survival.

DM occurs when insulin production (by the pancreas) is inadequate or the body's cells fail to respond to insulin properly. This results in an inability to absorb the glucose, causing high blood levels and subsequently glucose in the urine.

The most common clinical signs are excessive drinking and urination, increased appetite and weight loss, although coat changes and lethargy may also occur. If left untreated, it can progress to blindness caused by cataracts or further to a diabetic coma. Treatment is comparable to that for humans, with daily insulin injections for life.

and doesn't cause blindness. There may be some evidence of inherited cataracts in English Springers and these will be seen in younger dogs.

Retina: The retina is the layer at the back of the eye that receives light rays and is composed of cells called rods and cones. Rods aid vision in low light and cones help determine different colours; dogs' eyes are especially plentiful in rods compared to humans', hence better in lower light levels but not in colour. English Springer Spaniels can suffer from several retinal disorders (see Hereditary Disorders).

Cornea: The cornea is the transparent layer at the front of the eye that allows light to enter. With their inherent need to work every bit of undergrowth, English Springers may occasionally damage the cornea. **Trauma** to the cornea can result in tear production, blinking and pain, and, if untreated, may progress to infection and ulceration. **Ulceration**

Eyes should be bright and sparkling with no hint of soreness or discharge.

English Springer Spaniels appear to be predisposed to this disorder, and, as a result, may have an increased incidence of infection and ulceration of the cornea. Treatment, if needed, is usually in the form of lifelong artificial tears.

Gastrointestinal disorders

Foreign bodies: All dogs like to play with toys (and what they think are their toys but, in fact, are the family heirlooms!) and to feel the sensation of new substances with their mouths. English Springers have also been known to swallow the toy in question, potentially causing the intestine to become either partially or completely obstructed. Blockages in the intestinal tract can result in anorexia, vomiting, abdominal pain or diarrhoea. The degree of severity of clinical signs usually depends on the degree and duration of obstruction. If a blockage has occurred, the only option is surgery to remove the obstruction.

is where some of the cornea is damaged, often accompanied by conjunctivitis. If superficial then this may be treated with medicated eye drops, but if the injury persists or the initial ulcer is deeper, then there is a risk of rupture of the eye.

Conjunctivitis is the term for inflammation, discomfort and reddening of the conjunctiva (tissues around the eye). There are many causes of conjunctivitis – from bacterial or viral to trauma. Any sign of conjunctivitis could potentially be serious, requiring veterinary attention. **Dry eye** is the term applied to an inadequate tear film and drying of the conjunctiva and cornea.

Intestinal intussusception: This is where the intestine folds in on itself, often caused by hypermotility (excessive gut movement), to form a double tube that constricts, causing obstruction. Obstruction may initially be partial and proceed to complete. This condition is more common in young dogs aged six to eight months, with clinical signs being

Some Springers are natural scavengers, and this can lead to gastric upset.

vomiting, abdominal pain, anorexia and diarrhoea, occasionally with blood. Surgery is needed to remove any damaged intestine.

Gastritis: This is the inflammation of the stomach lining, typically resulting in vomiting. There are multiple causes, with scavenging usually high on the list of probabilities. Vomiting is the body's natural defence against poisoning and occasionally dogs may eat grass to bring on vomiting if they feel nauseous. Single episodes of vomiting are often seen and are not a problem in the dog as long as he remains bright and well. If vomiting continues or your dog appears unwell, a trip to the vet will be needed.

Diarrhoea: There are many reasons for diarrhoea. Often frequency of defecation increases and there may be blood or mucus present.

Sometimes a simple 24-hour withdrawal of food can be enough to clear any upset. At other times the condition can be life threatening. If your English Springer is unwell or off colour; if he is vomiting, or blood is noted in the faeces, veterinary advice should be sought.

Common causes of diarrhoea

Dietary: Any dog owner will know that all dogs at some point eat something that would not normally be considered on a menu! Rubbish bins raided by your Springer may contain unsavoury and potentially poisonous items. Therefore, bins inside and outside the house should be well secured. Sudden diet changes can upset the normal intestinal microflora so any diet alteration should be carried out over a four- to five-day period, gradually increasing the amount of the new diet.

**Bacterial infections *(Salmonella, Campylobacter, E. coli):* Care needs to be taken if these have been diagnosed, as they are potentially transmissible to humans, so strict hygiene methods should be employed to minimise the risks. Antibiotics are the mainstay of treatment, but severe cases may need hospitalisation.

Viral infections (canine distemper, canine parvovirus, coronavirus): These often require supportive

treatment, as there is rarely antiviral therapy available.

Parasites: A heavy worm burden may result in diarrhoea, and a regular worming regime should be employed to prevent them being a possible cause of any upset.

Enteritis: This is inflammation of the small intestine and again there is a long list of potential causes. Diarrhoea in large volumes with minimal straining occurs and may

Joint disorders

The bones and joints of all dogs are sensitive to physical trauma and disease, and even with four legs they occasionally manage to lose their footing and trip! Springer Spaniels live up to their name, being able to keep working until they (or you!) drop… which may occasionally result in trauma to the bones and joints.

Initial clinical signs that there may be a problem are lameness, stiffness and pain on movement. Usually a full physical examination and X-rays are necessary to help diagnose the problem. Any trauma to a joint will result in an increased susceptibility of that joint to succumb to arthritis later in life.

Osteoarthritis (OA): This degenerative joint disease results in the joints becoming enlarged, painful and stiff. Often seen in the older Springer

be seen with abdominal pain, dehydration, vomiting, anorexia and weight loss. Treatment is dependent on the cause, severity and duration of the disease.

Colitis: This is inflammation of the colon and can have multiple causes. Often diarrhoea is seen, which may be watery in consistency with either blood or mucus or both present. Repeated attempts to pass faeces are seen, with straining, often only producing small volumes. Treatment depends on the cause, severity and duration of disease.

Obesity
Physical fitness is a very important aspect of your dog's routine healthcare. English Springer Spaniels enjoy exercise and will work all day, but they can put on weight with age and a corresponding reduction in exercise. Obesity can have concerning medical effects, and with more dogs nowadays being overweight, a proportional increase

Spaniel, the first signs may be stiffness and slight lameness, especially after longer walks, which progress to a reluctance to exercise and severe lameness. There are many joint supplements and diets available to help slow progression of the disease, and pain-relieving medications can make your dog more comfortable in more severe cases. Ensuring that your English Springer does not put on weight in later years will reduce the load on the joints.

Hip dysplasia (HD): See Inherited Disorders

Osteochodrosis and osteochondritis dissecans (OCD): This is where there is inflammation and pain of the bone and cartilage, often due to abnormalities or trauma and the ensuing damage resulting in a flap of cartilage breaking off into the joint (known as 'joint mouse'). Occasionally seen in the younger, growing English Springer Spaniel, this can be a very painful condition, especially if the fragment moves within the joint, and surgery may be needed to remove it.

It is your responsibility to keep your English Springer at the correct weight.

in weight-related medical problems are also being noted.

- A high body-fat percentage increases anaesthetic and surgical risks.
- With increased body weight, there is more physical stress placed on the muscles, bones and joints and this can result in severe arthritis and joint problems in later life.
- Increased amounts of fat are also deposited around the internal organs, as in humans, and result in reduced function or dysfunction.
- Other medical diseases, such as diabetes, heart disease and breathing problems.

Regular exercise and a healthy diet are the magic ingredients to a fit and healthy dog. Treats can be high in fats and sugars, and should not be given on a regular basis. Using part of the daily diet ration is a good way to treat without increasing the calorific intake. Human food is often unsuitable for dogs and may be poisonous, so take care when giving scraps from your plate. There are specially formulated diets available to help with weight loss, but they need to be used together with increased exercise and a strict no-treats regime.

Skin conditions

English Springer Spaniels tend to have a soft, straight but weather-resistant coat and healthy skin. There are, however, a few conditions that can affect them.

Atopy: This is an inherited predisposition to develop a hypersensitivity to environmental allergens (e.g. pollens, dust mites, moulds). Initial signs are localised licking, itching and reddening of skin and may progress to generalised self-trauma, secondary infection, scaling and crusting. Treatment can involve steroids, antibiotics and even desensitisation vaccines following skin testing to determine the causative allergen.

Ehler-Danlos syndrome: This is an extremely rare heritable condition found in English Springer Spaniels where the skin becomes hyperextensible (stretchy), thin, fragile and easily torn. There is no cure and treatment is supportive.

Food hypersensitivity: English Springers can also have reactions to allergens in food. This may result in chronic diarrhoea, intolerance of certain foods, itchy skin or sore ears. The clinical signs are often variable in severity and diagnosis involves lengthy and strict food trials.

Intertrigo: This is where the skin rubs, becoming red and moist, with an increased likelihood of developing

The English Springer needs regular grooming so you can keep a check on his skin.

Urinary problems

Urine is produced in the kidneys (by filtering blood), transported via the ureters (tubes) to the bladder, where it is stored before being passed through the urethra (a tube) to the penis or vagina and voided. Any abnormality of urine or the act of urination can indicate a problem at any point of the urinary tract. Your English Springer should always have free access to fresh water to help reduce the risk of problems. Clinical signs are often similar irrespective of the cause. Look for

infection. English Springers can suffer this in the folds of skin around the lips; the first sign often being an extremely unpleasant smell, although it is not always easy to tell just where the smell is coming from! Useful preventative measures include keeping the hair in the lip-fold area clipped as short as possible and keeping the area dry. Cleansing shampoos will also help to keep skin dry, but antibiotics may be needed if infection occurs. In severe cases, surgical removal of the lip fold is usually very successful.

Interdigital dermatitis: English Springer Spaniels can suffer from irritated skin between their toes due to the large number of hairs growing

there. This can lead to excessive licking, skin trauma and infection. Grass seeds may penetrate the skin around the toes and can migrate up the leg, becoming very painful and infected. Bathing and antibiotics are usually sufficient to keep infection under control, although surgery may be required to remove the offending grass seed.

Tumours: Springers can suffer from some skin tumours as they get older – commonly benign but occasionally malignant. Any lumps or bumps that you notice should be examined by your vet, who may advise taking a sample to be checked by a pathologist to determine treatment.

straining or repeated attempts to pass urine; difficult, slow or painful urination; incontinence and abnormally strong-smelling or dark-coloured urine. If you notice any of these then, if possible, collect a fresh sample in a clean glass jar and take it with you to the veterinary surgery so they can analyse it after examining your dog.

The more common problems include:
• Bacterial cystitis
• Bladder stones (uroliths)
• Renal failure
• Tumours
• Incontinence.

MISCELLANEOUS

Rage syndrome

Mention is often made of cases of sudden uncharacteristic aggression, initially noted in Cocker Spaniels, but also in English Springer Spaniels and other breeds, which became widely known as rage syndrome. An affected dog suffers sudden, unpredictable bursts of severe aggression, during which he does not appear to know what he is doing and afterwards returns just as quickly to normal.

The cause of this condition has never been conclusively established although a number of theories have been suggested, such as a form of epilepsy. True cases of 'rage' are rare and most cases of aggression are due to other causes (health issues, lack of training, poor handling, insufficient exercise, inappropriate lifestyle, frustration etc.). If you are worried that your Springer Spaniel is suffering from rage syndrome, first consult your vet for a full examination to rule out a physical health problem, and, if all is well, seek referral to an experienced, qualified behaviourist.

INHERITED AND BREED-DISPOSED DISORDERS

The English Springer Spaniel does have a few breed-related disorders. If diagnosed with any of these diseases listed below, it is important to remember that they can affect offspring, so breeding from affected dogs should be discouraged.

The English Springer Spaniel is a breed without exaggeration and consequently suffers few breed specific disorders.

The British Veterinary Association (BVA), the Kennel Club (KC) and the International Sheep Dog Society (ISDS) have set up various screening tests in the UK to enable breeders to check for affected individuals and hence reduce the prevalence of these diseases within the breed.

DNA testing is now becoming more widely available, and, as research into the different genetic diseases progresses, more DNA tests are being developed.

Generalised Progressive Retinal Atrophy (GPRA)

GPRA is a bilateral degenerative disease of the retina, leading initially to night blindness and progressing to complete loss of vision. Normally seen in dogs aged four to five years, it may be seen as young as two years. Clinical identification is by examination of the eye, and the BVA/CK/ISDS Eye Scheme aims to identify affected individuals.

There is also a DNA test available to find the PRA – Cord1 mutation. A simple blood sample or cheek swab can be tested to determine whether a dog is normal (clear), a carrier of the condition or affected. Carrier dogs will never develop the disease but can produce affected dogs if mated to other carriers. The DNA

Retinal Pigment Epithelial Dystrophy (RPED)

RPED, previously called centralised progressive retinal atrophy (CPRA), is where an accumulation of pigment occurs in the retina. This causes a slowly progressive loss of vision, although not all dogs will become completely blind. There may be some link between RPED and vitamin E deficiency, and supplementation may prove helpful in preventing progression of the disease. There is a BVA/KC/ISDS Eye Scheme available for this condition; affected individuals are determined by an eye examination.

test means that breeders can identify carriers before breeding and can manage breeding programmes accordingly.

Goniodysgenesis/Primary Glaucoma

Goniodysgenesis is an inherited condition in English Springer Spaniels, also known as angle closure glaucoma. This is where there is abnormal development of the eye so that fluid that is constantly being produced within the eye (aqueous humour) cannot drain adequately. This, over time (can be very sudden), results in an increase in pressure within the eye, damaging the retina and resulting in clinical signs of acute conjunctivitis and pain.

Medication alone is not usually enough to treat and surgery is often indicated to relieve the pressure. The gonioscopy test is used to detect for predisposition to glaucoma under the BVA/KC/ISDS Eye Scheme.

Canine fucosidosis

This disease is caused by the absence of the enzyme alpha-L-fucosidase, which is essential for the breakdown of larger molecules into smaller ones. Without this breakdown process, the larger molecules accumulate in the body organs. Accumulation in the brain and peripheral nerves results in the clinical manifestation of the disease.

Clinical signs are generally evident from six months onwards with inco-ordination, loss of balance, changes in temperament, hearing or visual deficits, difficulties swallowing and possible seizures. Clinical signs worsen with time and, with no effective treatment available, this disease is ultimately fatal. There is a DNA test available to determine clear, affected or carrier individuals and as a means of diagnosis.

Phosphofructokinase (PFK) deficiency
PFK is an enzyme that helps in the conversion of sugar into energy in cells. Deficiency in this enzyme results in low sugar levels in some cells, such as red blood cells and muscle cells. Clinical signs are dark-coloured urine, pale gums, jaundice, fever and poor appetite, which may be worse after strenuous exercise (muscle cramps and weakness). Clinical signs may vary from mild to life-threatening with emergency attention needed.

There is no specific treatment available, but the disease can be managed by reducing exercise and

Multifocal Retinal Dysplasia

Retinal dysplasia is the abnormal development of the retina. The mildest form results in folds and rosettes (round clumps) seen as lines and stripes in the retina, with minimal effect on vision. More severe forms may manifest as complete retinal detachment and blindness, occasionally with associated cataracts and glaucoma. Retinal dysplasia is identified by an eye examination.

stress levels and thereby reducing numbers of red blood cells destroyed. DNA tests are available to determine whether a dog is clear, affected or a carrier.

Hip dysplasia

This is where the ball-and-socket joint of the hip develops incorrectly so that the head of the femur (ball) and the acetabulum of the pelvis (socket) do not fit snugly. This causes pain in the joint and may be seen as lameness in dogs as young as five months old with deterioration into severe arthritis over time. Gentle exercise, reduction in obesity, anti-inflammatory drugs and home management are all part of the treatment regimes used to control the disease.

English Springer Spaniels are prone to HD and the BVA/KC HD Scheme available involves the veterinary surgeon taking X-rays once a dog is over 12 months of age and sending them to the BVA. Here a 'hip score', ranging from a possible perfect 0 to a worst case 106 total, is allocated, determining the severity of disease. Dogs with scores under the breed mean standard should be used for breeding to improve the overall standard in future generations.

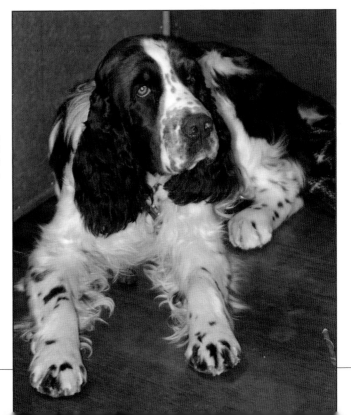

Exercise must be regulated if a dog shows signs of hip dysplasia.

IMHA and IMTP

Immune-mediated Haemolytic Anaemia (IMHA) and Immune-mediated Thrombocytopaenia (IMTP) are conditions where the body's immune system sees the red blood cells (IMHA) or platelets (IMTP) in the bloodstream as foreign and destroys them. English Springer Spaniels appear to have a predisposition to this disease.

Presentation of clinical signs of IMHA can vary from mild to severe anaemia with chronic to acute onset and life-threatening collapse due to the reduced oxygen-carrying capacity of the blood. IMTP may present with signs of increased bleeding as platelets are part of the clotting process. Often seen primarily as small bruises in the skin, large haemorrhages can occur internally, resulting in death from blood loss.

Both of these conditions may be managed medically with immuno-suppressive medications, but repeated blood transfusions may be necessary if severe.

Incomplete ossification of the humeral condyle

This is a condition found in English Springer Spaniels where the cartilage growth plate of the humerus (bone from shoulder to elbow) fails to ossify and mature at the elbow joint, resulting in a line of weakness. This line can easily fracture even with minimal stress (such as normal exercise) being placed on it.

Breeders strive to eliminate inherited disorders from their breeding programmes.

There may be no clinical signs of this abnormal development, or there may be severe pain and lameness in one or both of the forelimbs seen from a young age. X-rays will help diagnose the condition and surgery is indicated once fracture has occurred. Surgery and/or bone grafts may also help to stabilise the joint before a fracture occurs if the condition is detected early enough.

The affected joint is likely to develop osteoarthritis later in life and careful management regarding exercise and weight regimes, along with joint supplements and anti-inflammatories, can be used to help reduce ensuing pain.

SUMMING UP

It may give the pet owner cause for concern to find out about health problems that may affect their dog. But it is important to bear in mind that acquiring some basic knowledge is an asset, as it will allow you to spot any signs of

We are fortunate that that the English Springer is a hardy breed, and should live a long, happy and healthy life.

trouble at an early stage. Early diagnosis is very often the means to the most effective treatment.

Fortunately, the English Springer Spaniel is a generally healthy and disease-free dog, and, in most cases, owners can look forward to enjoying many happy years with this bouncing and carefree companion.

Useful Addresses

BREED & KENNEL CLUBS
Please contact your Kennel Club to obtain contact information about breed clubs in your area.

UK
The Kennel Club (UK)
1 Clarges Street London, W1J 8AB
Telephone: 0870 606 6750
Fax: 0207 518 1058
Web: www.thekennelclub.org.uk

USA
American Kennel Club (AKC)
5580 Centerview Drive, Raleigh, NC 27606.
Telephone: 919 233 9767
Fax: 919 233 3627
Email: info@akc.org
Web: www.akc.org

United Kennel Club (UKC)
100 E Kilgore Rd, Kalamazoo,
MI 49002-5584, USA.
Tel: 269 343 9020
Fax: 269 343 7037
Web:www.ukcdogs.com/

AUSTRALIA
Australian National Kennel Council (ANKC)
The Australian National Kennel Council is the administrative body for pure breed canine affairs in Australia. It does not, however, deal directly with dog exhibitors, breeders or judges. For information pertaining to breeders, clubs or shows, please contact the relevant State or Territory Body.

Dogs Australian Capital Teritory
PO Box 815, Dickson ACT 2602
Tel: (02) 6241 4404
Fax: (02) 6241 1129
Email: administrator@dogsact.org.au
Web: www.dogsact.org.au

Dogs New South Wales
PO Box 632, St Marys, NSW 1790
Tel: (02) 9834 3022 or 1300 728 022 (NSW Only)
Fax: (02) 9834 3872
Email: info@dogsnsw.org.au
Web: www.dogsnsw.org.au

Dogs Northern Territory
PO Box 37521, Winnellie NT 0821
Tel: (08) 8984 3570
Fax: (08) 8984 3409
Email: admin@dogsnt.com.au
Web: www.dogsnt.com.au

Dogs Queensland
PO Box 495, Fortitude Valley Qld 4006
Tel: (07) 3252 2661
Fax: (07) 3252 3864

Email: info@dogsqueensland.org.au
Web: www.dogsqueensland.org.au

Dogs South Australia
PO Box 844, Prospect East SA 5082
Tel: (08) 8349 4797
Fax: (08) 8262 5751
Email: info@dogssa.com.au
Web: www.dogssa.com.au

Tasmanian Canine Association Inc
The Rothman Building
PO Box 116, Glenorchy Tas 7010
Tel: (03) 6272 9443
Fax: (03) 6273 0844
Email: tca@iprimus.com.au
Web: www.tasdogs.com

Dogs Victoria
Locked Bag K9, Cranbourne VIC 3977
Tel: (03)9788 2500
Fax: (03) 9788 2599
Email: office@dogsvictoria.org.au
Web: www.dogsvictoria.org.au

Dogs Western Australia
PO Box 1404, Canning Vale WA 6970
Tel: (08) 9455 1188
Fax: (08) 9455 1190
Email: k9@dogswest.com
Web: www.dogswest.com

INTERNATIONAL
Fédération Cynologique Internationalé (FCI)
Place Albert 1er, 13, B-6530 Thuin, Belgium.
Tel: +32 71 59.12.38
Fax: +32 71 59.22.29
Web: www.fci.be/

TRAINING AND BEHAVIOUR

UK
Association of Pet Dog Trainers
Telephone: 01285 810811
Web: http://www.apdt.co.uk

Association of Pet Behaviour Counsellors
Telephone: 01386 751151
Web: http://www.apbc.org.uk/

USA
Association of Pet Dog Trainers
Tel: 1 800 738 3647
Web: www.apdt.com/

American College of Veterinary Behaviorists
Web: http://dacvb.org/

American Veterinary Society of Animal Behavior
Web: www.avsabonline.org/

AUSTRALIA
APDT Australia Inc
Web: www.apdt.com.au

Canine Behaviour
For details of regional behvaiourists, contact the
relevant State or Territory Controlling Body.

ACTIVITIES

UK
Agility Club
http://www.agilityclub.co.uk/

British Flyball Association
Telephone: 01628 829623
Web: http://www.flyball.org.uk/

USA
North American Dog Agility Council
Web: www.nadac.com/

North American Flyball Association, Inc.
Tel/Fax: 800 318 6312
Web: www.flyball.org/

AUSTRALIA
Agility Dog Association of Australia
Tel: 0423 138 914
Web: www.adaa.com.au/

NADAC Australia (North American Dog Agility
Council - Australian Division)
Web: www.nadacaustralia.com/

Australian Flyball Association
Tel: 0407 337 939
Web: www.flyball.org.au/

INTERNATIONAL
World Canine Freestyle Organisation
Tel: (718) 332-8336
Web: www.worldcaninefreestyle.org

HEALTH

UK
Alternative Veterinary Medicine Centre
Tel: 01367 710324
Web: www.alternativevet.org/

British Small Animal Veterinary Association
Tel: 01452 726700
Web: http://www.bsava.com/

Royal College of Veterinary Surgeons
Tel: 0207 222 2001
Web: www.rcvs.org.uk

USA
American Holistic Veterinary Medical Association
Tel: 410 569 0795
Web: www.ahvma.org/

American Veterinary Medical Association
Tel: 800 248 2862
Web: www.avma.org

American College of Veterinary Surgeons
Tel: 301 916 0200

Toll Free: 877 217 2287
Web: www.acvs.org/

AUSTRALIA
Australian Holistic Vets
Web: www.ahv.com.au/

Australian Small Animal Veterinary Association
Tel: 02 9431 5090
Web: www.asava.com.au

Australian Veterinary Association
Tel: 02 9431 5000
Web: www.ava.com.au

Australian College Veterinary Scientists
Tel: 07 3423 2016
Web: http://acvsc.org.au

ASSISTANCE DOGS

UK
Canine Partners
Tel: 08456 580480
Web: www.caninepartners.co.uk

Dogs for the Disabled
Tel: 01295 252600
Web: www.dogsforthedisabled.org

Guide Dogs for the Blind Association
Tel: 01189 835555
Web: www.guidedogs.org.uk/

Hearing Dogs for Deaf People
Tel: 01844 348100
Web: www.hearingdogs.org.uk

Pets as Therapy
Tel: 01845 345445
Web: http://www.petsastherapy.org/

Support Dogs
Tel: 01142 617800
Web: www.support-dogs.org.uk

USA
Therapy Dogs International
Tel: 973 252 9800
Web: www.tdi-dog.o

Therapy Dogs Inc.
Tel: 307 432 0272.
Web: www.therapydogs.com

Delta Society - Pet Partners
Web: www.deltasociety.org

Comfort Caring Canines
Web: www.comfortcaringcanines.org/

AUSTRALIA
AWARE Dogs Australia, Inc
Tel: 07 4093 8152
Web: www.awaredogs.org.au/

Delta Society — Therapy Dogs
Web: www.deltasociety.com.au

About The Authors

JULIETTE CUNLIFFE
Juliette Cunliffe has been involved with dogs for more than 30 years, during which time she has exhibited show dogs with considerable success. Also a caring breeder and Championship Show Judge, she awards Challenge Certificates in four breeds, with others on the near horizon. She judges extensively abroad where her expertise, and also her lectures on dogs, are in high demand.

Greatly interested in all breeds, with a particular penchant for canine history, she has written a number of dog books, several of which have been translated into other languages. She also writes regularly for the dog press both in the UK and overseas.

ESTELA BADEN **BSc Hons BVSc MRCVS**
Estela graduated as a veterinary surgeon from Liverpool University in 2006. Since qualifying she has been working in a small animal practice in Monmouthshire. Whilst interested in all aspects of small animal practice, she has particular interests in small animal surgery and animal behaviour.
See Chapter Six: Health Care for the English Springer Spaniel.

Further Reading

English Springer Spaniel
(BEST OF BREED)

Written by leading experts, including Celia Woodbridge, *The English Springer Spaniel* offers readers an unrivalled depth of knowledge about their chosen breed. The book gives detailed information on character and behaviour, puppy care, training and socialisation, with a special chapter on English Springer health written by a practising vet. Illustrated by a stunning collection of more than 120 specially-commissioned colour photographs, matched by the high-specification production, and distinctively finished with real cloth binding, this is one breed book no Spinger lover should be without.

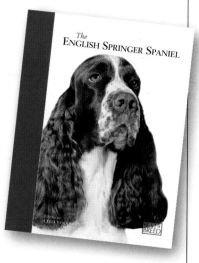

*Available in the UK from Corpus Publishing,
The Granary, Bishton Farm, Tidenham, Chepstow,
Gloucestershire NP16 7LJ
Price: £14.99 (plus £2 p+p)*

Index